Native Plants
IN THE HOME LANDSCAPE

FOR
THE
UPPER
MIDWEST

Keith Gerard Nowakowski

UNIVERSITY OF ILLINOIS
EXTENSION
CIRCULAR 1381

UNIVERSITY OF ILLINOIS
EXTENSION

College of Agricultural, Consumer
and Environmental Sciences
UNIVERSITY OF ILLINOIS AT URBANA-CHAMPAIGN

Issued in furtherance of Cooperative Extension Work, Acts of May 8 and June 30, 1914, in cooperation with the U.S. Department of Agriculture. Robert Hoeft, Interim Director, University of Illinois Extension. University of Illinois Extension provides equal opportunities in programs and employment.

See page 120 for additional credits.

Contents

TOP: PRAIRIE TRILLIUM (*Trillium recurvatum*)

BELOW, LEFT: FRAGRANT SUMAC (*Rhus aromatica*)

BELOW, RIGHT: KALM'S ST. JOHNS-WORT (*Hypericum kalmianum*)

Acknowledgments

ALTHOUGH I HAVE BEEN AN AVID GARDENER and plantsman for more than 25 years, the world of native landscaping is a relatively new fascination for me. I would like to thank the following people for their encouragement, their time, the wealth of information that they hold, and their generosity in sharing it with me.

Thank you to University of Illinois professors Gary Kessler, Dianne Harris, Amida Sinha, and Dianne Noland for helping me flesh out an outline and focus for this project, as well as reviewing the resulting product.

To the many members of the North Park Village Chapter of the Wild Ones, the Grand Prairie Friends of Illinois, and the Illinois Native Plant Society, I would like to offer my thanks to all who helped answer my questions on plant care and use and who encouraged me to complete this project.

I would like to thank homeowners Don and Maureen Carlson, Jim and Joan DeHorn, Linda Dynek, Kathy Greenholdt, Marianne Hahn, Steven Hill, John Marlin, Jim and Mare Payne, Conner Shaw, Paul Tessene, and Marian and John Thill for kindly inviting me to their homes and giving me the grand tour of their naturally landscaped yards.

Thanks to the many Illinois Natural History Survey specialists who came to my assistance, including Steven Hill, Mike Jeffords, Ken Robertson, John Taft, and Paul Tessene.

To Mike Jeffords, Gary Kling, Bob Reber, Ken Robertson, and Denny Schrock for providing some of the photographic images used in this book.

To Linda Dynek, of Loba Landscapes, a natural landscape designer in Batavia, Illinois, for discussing the possibilities of using native plants in the designed landscape.

To Guy Sternberg, author of *Landscaping with Native Trees, The Northeast, Midwest, Midsouth and Southeast Edition,* for answering my questions on tree culture.

To Marianne Hahn, friend and president of the Midewin Tallgrass Prairie Alliance, for introducing me to the wonderful sand savannas of Kankakee County, Illinois, and for sharing with me her knowledge of plant identification and prairie restoration.

To Dwain Berggren, steward of Loda Prairie, for giving me a tour of the remnant cemetery prairie in east-central Illinois and for offering his assistance in answering my questions as I worked on this project.

To Bob Porter, president of the North Park Village Chapter of the Wild Ones, for allowing me time to present this project to the Wild Ones members in the early stages and ask for their feedback on my proposed plant list.

Thank you also to the following nurserymen:

Jeff Sayre, director of operations, and Mark O'Brian, head of sales and marketing for J.F. New and Associates native plant nursery in Walkerton, Indiana, for showing me around their greenhouse operations, cold room, and growing fields and for offering assistance in answering my questions.

Conner Shaw, owner of Possibility Place Nursery in Monee, Illinois, for giving me a tour of his operation, which specializes in growing oaks as well as other native trees and shrubs, and for discussing the usefulness of this project.

Steve Banovetz of Agrecol Corporation, in Sun Prairie, Wisconsin, and Roy Diblik of Northwind Perennial Farm in Lyons, Wisconsin, for fielding my questions on plant culture.

I would like to offer my appreciation to librarians Beth Wohlgemuth and JoAnn Jacoby, of the Illinois Natural History Survey Library, for their enthusiastic assistance in helping me find the research material I needed to complete this project.

And a special thanks to my thesis committee—the chairman, professor Bill Sullivan, and committee members, professors Gary Kling and Denny Schrock, for their oversight and encouragement during the writing process.

Introduction

GETTING TO KNOW AND ENJOY the beauty of prairie plants is an exciting and fulfilling adventure. You may have gardened all your life and enjoyed the magnificence of prairie or woodland wildflowers on your visits to the local nature preserve, never thinking about how or if these interesting plants could be used in your own home landscape. Increasingly though, you have probably heard about or seen others using these plants around their homes, while wondering how you could become familiar enough with their culture and habits to use them in a well-designed landscape of your own—a landscape that doesn't look like a weed patch or offend the neighbors but allows you to enjoy its unique beauty and the birds and butterflies it attracts. These questions and concerns are the reason this book was written—to help anyone interested in learning more about midwestern plants, their culture, and potential uses in the designed home landscape.

So few people seem to know about plants native to the Midwest, plants such as Prairie Smoke, Blue-Eyed Grass, Bloodroot, Staghorn Sumac, or Hophornbeam. This is a shame but not surprising. Much of these plants' native habitat has been converted to agricultural or residential use; they are rarely promoted on gardening shows or available at nurseries. Historically, these plants have been overlooked as possible candidates for use in the home landscape in favor of imports from Europe and Asia. With names that often incorporate the words *wild*, *common*, or *weed*, who would think of them as ornamentals? Fortunately, increasing numbers of people are recognizing their ornamental qualities as well as their environmental attributes. These people want dynamic landscapes that offer them a reason to get out in their yards other than to mow the lawn or trim the hedge. This book is intended as a guide to help you through the process of designing just such a landscape.

Unlike most home landscapes, a landscape that takes its inspiration from surrounding wild areas is more than just a disparate mix of plants. It is a community of plants that reflect the natural heritage of the region. In chapter one, "A Tallgrass Prairie Timeline," a review of this heritage is presented. The tallgrass prairie is a relatively young ecosystem, dating back only to the end of the Great Ice Age about 10,000 years ago; but the conditions that created, maintained, and ultimately destroyed the tallgrass prairie are fascinating and helpful in appreciating the remnants that are still around.

In chapter two, "The Benefits of Using Wildflowers and Other Native Plants," some advantages of regional landscaping are discussed. A home landscape that incorporates adapted regional plants and reduces the area devoted to lawn has much to recommend it over conventional landscape design. Once the plants are established, maintenance is less tedious, irrigation is eliminated, fertilizers and pesticides are not needed, diversity of life is increased, seasonal change in the landscape is observed, and a sense of place is established. These benefits and more are soon realized with properly chosen plant material.

There are, however, many choices to consider when thinking about regional design; how do you begin to narrow the range of possibilities? Chapter three, "Where Do I Begin?" explains how visiting nearby nature preserves and getting to know the plants growing there, as well as evaluating your own yard and your individual needs, can help you create a landscape that takes its inspiration from these natural areas while containing plants that suit you, your yard, and your neighbors.

In chapter four, "Plants of the Tallgrass Region," more than 80 plant species, including trees, shrubs, wildflowers, ferns, sedges, and grasses native to the tallgrass prairie region, are described, including their culture and how they might be used in the designed home landscape. These plants were chosen for their visual appeal, multiple seasons of interest, ease of culture, commercial availability, and suitability to a small site. With the same care that should be given to any good landscape design, a yard containing these plants will put on a display that is hard to beat and will be the envy of your neighbors.

Getting you to remove all of your lawn (as well as other exotic plant material) and turning your yard into a wildflower meadow is not the intent of this book. Nor is that approach usually the most attractive option in a small yard. Municipal weed laws should not even be an issue with our approach. Simply reduce the area devoted to lawn, and incorporate these natives into planting beds as you would any exotic plant from Europe or Asia. Chapter five, "Landscape Designs with Nature in Mind," offers a few examples.

The success of your new landscape, however, depends on how, when, and where you install your plants, as well as how well you maintain them. In chapter six, "Installing and Maintaining Your Home Landscape," some basic tasks involved in preparing, installing, and maintaining your landscape are reviewed. Proper handling and care of your plant can help them become established in their new homes more quickly and allows you to enjoy their many benefits sooner.

I hope that this book entices you to look at your yard with new eyes, that it encourages you to explore alternatives to the status quo in landscape design, and that you use these ideas not only in your backyard but in areas visible from the street as well. As Michael Pollan wrote in "Beyond Wilderness and Lawn" *(Harvard Design,* Winter/Spring 1998), "Gardening, as a cultural activity, matters deeply, not only to the look of our landscape, but also to the wisdom of our thinking about the environment."

CHAPTER ONE

A Tallgrass Prairie Timeline

THE STORY BEHIND the rise of the tallgrass prairie and its dominance of the central North American landscape for thousands of years, as well as its ultimate disappearance, is an interesting one. Formed as the result of glaciers and a warming climate, maintained by fire and other disturbances, and turned under by the plow to become the richest farmland in the world, the tallgrass prairie reveals a landscape with a rich and intriguing past.

The Great Ice Age and Prairie Formation

During the Pleistocene Epoch, otherwise known as the Great Ice Age, much of North America was covered by a series of advancing and receding ice sheets, or glaciers. During the most recent glacial event, spanning 75,000 to 10,000 years ago, the Wisconsinan, an ice sheet a mile or more thick, reached as far south as what is now New York City, across to St. Louis, and west to Seattle. The Wisconsinan, along with its predecessor, the Illinoian, is largely responsible for the extreme flatness of most of Illinois, as well as the rolling ridges in the northeastern part of the state.

The Illinoian glacier extended as far south as Carbondale, Illinois, 300,000 to 125,000 years ago, farther south than any other glacier in North America, flattening much of Illinois in the process. The Wisconsinan glacial event did not advance as far, reaching only the northeastern and central parts of Illinois. But it was responsible for the formation of the Great Lakes; and because, at one point, its front edge was melting at the same rate that it was moving forward, it left behind a series of ridges, or glacial moraines, made up of rocky debris.

The Wisconsinan ice sheet began its retreat northward after major—and sudden—climatic changes occurred 12,000 years ago. The earth's temperature was warming, and ocean levels began to rise. As the ice receded, the resulting midwestern landscape initially looked much like the Alaskan Arctic does today, with expanses of tundra and spruce forests, rather than the grasslands encountered by early European settlers. With increasing temperatures, these spruce forests were replaced by Jack, Red, and White Pines, as well as deciduous trees such as birch, elm, Blue Beech, hickory, and oak—species of cool, moist forests. As the climate continued to become warmer and drier, oaks and hickories, species that were better adapted to these new conditions, became the dominant trees. But even these remaining trees could outcompete the prairie only along waterways, creating a band that varied from 1 to 6, up to 12, miles wide, where the eroded soils favored tree growth. Prairies prevailed on the broad, flat landscape, where fine, wind-blown silt known as loess covered the rocky glacial till, reaching their maximum dominance 7,000 years ago.

Prairie Resilience

Although major climatic events many thousands of years ago promoted the creation and spread of the tallgrass prairie, a combination of several factors since its formation (including weather and fire), in association with the geography of the region, played key roles in keeping it the dominant landscape feature in the thousands of years since its formation.

WEATHER

In the upper Midwest, weather patterns create a unique set of climatic conditions that favor the growth of prairie grasses and wildflowers. These plants are well adapted to the extremes in temperature from summer to winter, extended droughts, and dry winter winds common to the region. The tallgrass prairie, rather than other forms of vegetation, existed in part because of these weather-related stresses.

A person traveling from the East Coast west to the Great Plains would notice the landscape change from forest to tallgrass prairie (now mostly corn and soybeans) and ultimately to shortgrass prairie. A significant reason for this change, from east to west, is the amount of moisture held in the soil and made available for plant growth throughout the growing season.

East of the tallgrass prairie region, there is an increase in rainfall due to moisture-laden air masses coming down from the Arctic as well as up from the Gulf Coast—air masses that only erratically bring precipitation to the Midwest. This increase in moisture, as well as other factors such as the East's more mountainous geography, favors forest cover. To the west, on the Great Plains, the Rocky Mountains cause a decrease in rainfall, creating a drier, more arid climate; there, shortgrass prairie and mesquite grasslands dominate the landscape.

Soil moisture and humidity levels in the tallgrass prairie region itself are the result of predominately dry, westerly winds in the winter and short but intense storms that come up from the Gulf of Mexico in the summer. These storms are often so intense that rainwater runs off before it has time to soak into the ground. Also, periods of drought in the prairie region are not uncommon and can last for months or years, killing many trees (both young and mature specimens) but only causing grasses and wildflowers to go dormant until conditions improve, thereby allowing prairie to become reestablished in previously forested areas.

PRAIRIE DROPSEED (*Sporobolus heterolepis*)

FIRE

The particular climate of the Midwest, however, was not the sole reason for the existence of the tallgrass prairie; fire played an equal, if not more important, role in its dominance. The open, gently rolling surface of the prairie, its cover of dense grass, high winds, and periods of drought all combined to foster widespread fires. And fires were known to have routinely swept across a dry expanse of prairie, killing most trees and shrubs in their path but burning only the dried tops of prairie grasses and wildflowers—plants well adapted to periodic burns, able to resprout later in spring due to their deep and massive root systems, as well as their protected underground growing points. Fires were started either by natural causes such as lightning or by American Indians, who set prairie fires in their effort to herd bison for hunting. Today, controlled fires in early spring or late autumn are used as a primary management tool in maintaining the quality of what little prairie remains in the Midwest. Fire removes the built-up layer of dead leaves and stems of grasses and wildflowers, exposing the soil surface to the warming effects of the springtime sun and returning nutrients to the soil.

Early Exploration and Settlement of the Prairie

*The scenery of the prairie country ... is striking, and never fails to cause
an exclamation of surprise. The extent of the prospect is exhilarating.
The line of the landscape is sloping and graceful. The verdure and flowers
are beautiful, and the absence of shade, and consequent appearance of a
profusion of light, produces a gaiety which animates the beholder.*

JAMES HALL, *Notes on the Western States*, 1838

Some of the first Europeans to travel the waterways of the upper Midwest were late-seventeenth-century French explorers and missionaries. When they encountered the area's seemingly endless grasslands, they where overwhelmed; and for lack of a more descriptive term, they referred to what they saw as "prairie," the French word for a grazed meadow. The grazers, which they called "wild cattle," were herds of bison roaming the grasslands some 60 million strong, in herds of up to 12 million.

The tallgrass prairie still covered a vast, roughly diamond-shaped area of central North America as recently as the early 1800s. Centered on Iowa, the prairie stretched from just over the border into Manitoba, Canada, southeast to the southern tip of Lake Michigan, south to Austin, Texas, and back up to west-central Nebraska. It was a sea of grasses up to 8 feet tall, grasslike sedges, and rushes, as well as numerous and varied flowering forbs, or wildflowers; this expanse was broken only occasionally by a grove of oaks or a line of trees along a waterway.

At first, settlers coming from the East in search of affordable farmland ignored the parcels of land covered in prairie, thinking the soils of the treeless grassland would not support their crops, and instead sought out and cleared the occasional grove of trees for their new homestead. The reverse, however, was soon found to be true; and the process of turning the fertile grassland into cropland began in earnest. By 1838, when author James Hall wrote about the region, Chicago was an incorporated city of 4,170 people; and John Deere, a blacksmith from Moline, Illinois, had introduced the steel moldboard plow to midwestern farmers only a year earlier. Before Deere's "self-scouring" plow came onto the scene, farmers had a difficult time cutting through the rich but often mucky soils of the tallgrass region with their easily fouled iron plows brought from the East Coast. Deere's plow increased a farmer's efficiency and made it feasible to turn large tracts of prairie into productive cropland to help feed a rapidly growing country. Thus marked the beginning of the end for the tallgrass prairie.

What had been prairie for 8,000 to 10,000 years in Illinois was almost totally lost to agriculture and other development by the year 1900. Wetlands were drained, streams straightened, woodlands cut for timber, and prairie grasses plowed under. By 1978, an Illinois Natural Areas Inventory showed that only one-hundredth of one percent of the original 22 million acres of Illinois prairie remained intact; and nationwide, over 90 percent of the original tallgrass prairie was gone.

NATIVE PLANTS IN THE HOME LANDSCAPE

CHAPTER TWO

The Benefits of Using Wildflowers and Other Native Plants

As our remaining wilderness areas become increasingly closed in and isolated by human development, it becomes ever more important that the landscapes surrounding our homes enhance rather than degrade our region's unique community of plants, animals, soils, and waters. Following are a few of the many benefits that are realized by reducing the area devoted to lawn and increasing the number of native plants used in the home landscape.

Diversity of Life

In *A Sand County Almanac*, ecologist Aldo Leopold wrote about the need for a "land ethic." He noted that "there is as yet no ethic dealing with man's relation to land and to the animals and plants which grow upon it." A land ethic, he said, "changes the role of *Homo sapiens* from conqueror of the land-community to plain member and citizen of it. It implies respect for his fellow-members, and also respect for the community as such." Fortunately, since the book's publication in 1949, there has been an increase in the awareness of, and concern for, how land use based solely on economic self-interest can have drastic consequences when it comes to the Earth's environmental health and its diversity of life.

By replacing at least part of your lawn, which is useless to most wildlife, with native shade trees, shrubs, wildflowers, and grasses, you can help reduce the cause and severity of these negative impacts on the environment. And by doing so, you are not only increasing the beauty and value of your home, you are also creating an environment that will help maintain a diversity of plants and animals on both the local and global scale.

Maintenance

Many home landscapes are maintained to look the same throughout the growing season and from year to year. To achieve this effect, the grass is mowed, irrigated, and fertilized; and sometimes, even herbicides and pesticides are called into action in an effort to maintain the

RED OSIER DOGWOOD (*Cornus stolonifera [C. sericea]*)

"perfect" lawn. Additionally, every spring the shrubs are trimmed back into architecturally pleasing forms, the plastic edging that popped out of the ground over winter is reinstalled, the leaves and twigs that fell into the rock mulch are removed, and a row of petunias is planted. It takes some work to keep a landscape static and sterile. However, replacing your manicured shrubs or part of your lawn with a prairie grass and wildflower garden may or may not reduce the amount of time you spend maintaining your yard's appearance.

Unwanted shoots from some native plants such as Red Osier Dogwood and Staghorn Sumac will need to be cut back to the ground, the occasional weed will still need to be hoed out, a topdressing of wood chips will need to be applied every few years, and any wildflowers that have popped up in areas where they are not wanted will need to be dug out and moved to another part of the yard or passed on to friends. But unlike most traditional landscapes, prairie gardens are dynamic; they are beautiful to look at, fun to be in, and exciting to explore. And pulling a few weeds or trimming back a shrub while checking out what has come into bloom and listening to the birds' songs of appreciation somehow makes these necessary chores more rewarding and enjoyable.

Irrigation

Lawns of Kentucky Bluegrass, a grass that is native to a cooler climate in Eurasia, take a lot of water to stay green throughout the growing season. In fact, in some urban areas on the East Coast, up to 30 percent of the water consumed, and up to 60 percent on the West Coast, is used to irrigate lawns. Unlike turfgrass, however, the prairie grasses and wildflowers described in this book actually thrive in the heat of the summer and need no supplemental watering to look great. In fact, if watered on a regular basis, these grasses and wildflowers may put on too much top growth for their stems to support, causing them to flop over ungracefully.

The trees and shrubs found in this book, while quite adaptable to various growing conditions, have particular requirements that favor their growth. Some—such as Black Tupelo, Sugar Maple, and Winterberry Holly—prefer consistent soil moisture and should never be planted in dry, sunny locations where irrigation would be necessary for their survival. On such a site, a combination of White Oak, Pasture Rose, and Hophornbeam would be a better choice. If properly chosen for the site, native plants should never require irrigation after the first year for them to thrive.

LEFT: PASTURE ROSE (*Rosa carolina*)
RIGHT: WINTERBERRY HOLLY (*Ilex verticillata*)

Fertilizer and Pesticide Use

With so much property devoted to lawn, homeowners actually apply more fertilizer and pesticide to their home landscape per acre than farmers apply to their crops. And because lawns are just slightly less impervious to water than is asphalt, these chemicals and nutrients do not penetrate deeply into the soil. Instead, they are commonly washed away during heavy rains, often finding their way into lakes and streams. The result is a reduction in water quality that can negatively affect both people and aquatic life.

The use of fertilizer and pesticides of any sort on prairie plants is neither necessary nor recommended. As it is, most prairie plants are rarely bothered by insect pests—due to a natural balance of predator and prey. And when plants are partially denuded, such as when monarch caterpillars gorge themselves on the leaves of a milkweed plant, it is rare for the long-term

PRAIRIE SMOKE (*Geum triflorum*)

NATIVE PLANTS IN THE HOME LANDSCAPE

vigor of plants to be negatively affected. Many insects, in fact, act as pollinators, benefiting both the plants and the birds that eat much of the seed produced. Other insects directly provide a source of food for songbirds, bats, and other wildlife. The use of pesticides disrupts this balance of predator and prey.

The use of fertilizers is also discouraged and seldom necessary with native plants. The roots of prairie grasses and wildflowers reach deep into the soil—an average of 4 to 6 feet—in search of nutrients; and the roots of legumes such as Leadplant and the Prairie Indigos, as well as the nonleguminous New Jersey Tea, have the useful ability to convert nitrogen from the air into a form that can be used by the plant. Ultimately, the plants put out as much top growth as their roots can support; and if fertilized, they may bush out, become taller, and perhaps produce a greater flower display, but the plants become crowded, stressed, and shorter-lived than if they were left unfertilized. This lush growth also requires more water to sustain it, something the roots cannot supply without supplemental watering, especially during times of drought. To keep your prairie garden healthy and carefree, do not fertilize it.

Seasonal Change

A well-designed and carefully thought out landscape using native plants is always changing and evolving throughout the growing season. In March and April, the woodland flowers first appear and put on their show under a canopy of Serviceberry and Redbud blooms. In May, the chartreuse flowers of Golden Alexanders contrast spectacularly with the electric blue flowers of Spiderwort, which are later complemented by the orange Butterfly Milkweed and pinkish Pale Purple Coneflower in June. This process of successive bloom continues through to autumn, when the grasses come to center stage in August and September, sending out their flower stalks and slowly turning shades of russet and gold as the days shorten. At the same time, the purple Aromatic Asters and bright yellow Stiff Goldenrods make their long-awaited appearance as the sumacs turn brilliant shades of red, orange, and yellow. And throughout all of this, birds can be observed chasing down insects, butterflies and hummingbirds are seen sipping nectar—while toads relax in the shade and monarch caterpillars gorge themselves at an all-you-can-eat milkweed buffet. There is always something interesting and new to discover when native plants are part of the landscape.

A Sense of Place

By using in your home landscape the plants that are commonly found in the tallgrass prairie region—such as Bur Oak, Smooth Sumac, and Stiff Goldenrod, rather than Norway Maple,

Dwarf Burning Bush, and Japanese Spirea—you are creating something that reflects the unique prairie landscape. Historically though, the plant material used around most homes has rarely reflected the region in which they are located. More often than not, a home located within the Lake Michigan dunelands of Indiana is landscaped exactly the same as one in central Illinois or for that matter in Denver, Colorado. They lack local color or "a sense of place."

One reason for these generic landscapes, which are ubiquitous across America, is that most people have traditionally thought of our region's prairie plants as weeds, something found along roadsides and in empty city lots or otherwise deemed inappropriate for use in the home landscape (such as the misconception that oak trees are slow growing or that goldenrod causes hay fever). Even many landscape designers are unfamiliar with native plants and their potential use in the home landscape. Fortunately though, as people have become aware of how dynamic and beautiful a prairie-style landscape can be, demand for native plants has increased. In reaction to this demand, there are increasing numbers of midwestern nurseries (see page 101) that specialize in growing prairie plants or are expanding their line of plant material to include native grasses, wildflowers, trees, and shrubs. Landscape designers as well are becoming aware of this demand by homeowners for more ecologically sound and interesting landscapes, landscapes that help to retain our region's biodiversity and offer a sense of place.

CHAPTER THREE

Where Do I Begin?

BEGIN YOUR PRAIRIE LANDSCAPE as you would most endeavors, by acquiring knowledge. Read books, browse nursery catalogs, visit natural areas, and join groups promoting conservation. When you are able to recognize many plants of the tallgrass prairie region by name and learn about their culture, usefulness to wildlife, and folklore (such as their historical use as food, medicine, and sources for dye), it becomes more exciting to acquire and grow them. Also, planning your landscape will be much simpler and more interesting when you know where certain plants occurred naturally and with what other plants they were associated. Were they plants of the sand dunes, river's edge, open prairie, or oak savanna? You can use these natural associations as a guide to what plants will grow and look well together under the existing conditions around your own home. Therefore, the best way to begin your prairie landscape is not by going out to your yard with a tape measure and shovel but by taking the time to learn as much as you can about the plants and their habitats. Then when you do go out to your yard, creative solutions to your landscape needs will come much more easily.

Gaining Knowledge Is Your First Step

INFORMATIONAL AND INSPIRATIONAL BOOKS

There are many great books to inspire you, nursery catalogs to inform you, and organizations to assist you in your quest for knowledge. Field guides can help with plant identification and sometimes with a plant's folklore and culture as well. A few of these guides that I found invaluable when learning about these plants are listed on page 109. But some of the most interesting books are the ones that inspire action and a desire to learn more, books such as Aldo Leopold's *A Sand County Almanac,* written by one of the first proponents for the conservation of prairies, debating that their value should not be considered solely in economic terms but rather in terms of the ecological greater good gained by their continued existence; Sara Stein's *Noah's Garden,* detailing the adventures of a homeowner who wants to bring nature into her yard; or May Watt's *Reading the Landscape,* offering insights on the cultural and natural heritage of the tallgrass prairie. These books, which are full of wonderful observations, are highly recommended as sources of inspiration as you begin or continue your journey into natural landscaping.

NURSERY CATALOGS

Another source of inspiration can be found in nursery catalogs specializing in prairie plants. Many catalogs contain great color pictures, and all offer useful information on how to use the plants in your landscape. In their pages, you can find out more about "no-mow" lawns or discover plant kits of wildflowers that are attractive to butterflies or hummingbirds or resistant to deer browsing, as well as kits with plants that do well in clay, dry, or wet soils, in full sun or part shade. There are benefits to purchasing these plant kits, such as the ease of acquiring a selection of grasses and wildflowers that do well under certain conditions or their having been developed to produce a show of flowers from spring until fall. But before purchasing a preselected mix of plants, be sure that their size and growth habits are visually suited to your landscape needs. Most mixes may perform as promoted, but the mix of plants could wind up looking more like a weed patch than a prairie if you are not careful. Often, it is better simply to use these mixes as a guide in selecting the individual plants that best suit your needs. See page 101 for a list by state of Midwest native plant nurseries.

LOCAL CONSERVATION GROUPS

As using native plants in the home landscape becomes more popular, you might be surprised at the number of people in your own community who are interested in or actively doing just that; and many of them belong to local conservation groups. These groups can be found by looking in your local paper, asking your librarian, or contacting your local Extension office—in Illinois, University of Illinois Extension, **www.extension.uiuc.edu** or **(217)333-5900**—to find out who might be holding native plant sales or when and where groups such as the Audubon Society or the Wild Ones (see page 111) with local chapters nationwide are holding their next meeting. You may also find groups that exist because of your area's unique regional landscape, groups such as the Friends of the Indiana Dunes in northern Indiana, the Grand Prairie Friends of Illinois, or the McHenry County Defenders in northeastern Illinois.

In addition to holding native plant sales, sponsoring lectures, or exploring natural areas, these groups often have Web sites full of information and links to other sites of interest (see page 111). Being a part of these groups not only allows you to meet people who can answer your questions about native plants while on field trips or at meetings but also, by actively supporting their efforts through membership dues as well as volunteering your time, helps to protect your region's remaining wild areas.

Getting to Know Your Local Native Landscape

Even though we refer to an area that covers several states as (what was) the "tallgrass prairie," this region did not consist of a monotonous repetition of the same grasses, wildflowers, trees, and shrubs. Rather, it was a complex of many distinct and varied ecologic systems, each containing a characteristic mix of plants. And though the tallgrass prairie no longer exists, remnants of these unique systems survive. Near your own home, there might be examples of dry, wet, or mesic (moist) prairies represented by hill, sand, or black-soil prairies. There may be wet bogs, fens, or marshes; dry dunes or oak–hickory woods; moist beech–maple woods and flatwoods, as well as sandy Black Oak savannas or Bur Oak savannas on heavier soils. Visiting these wild areas near your home, whether in nature preserves or along roadside and railroad track easements, and becoming familiar with their plant communities can be helpful when it comes to choosing plants for the landscape around your home. And by choosing native plants that can be found growing locally, you can create a landscape that reflects your area's natural heritage and help to extend the edges of these increasingly rare and isolated wild areas.

Taking Notes and Photographing What You See

As you read, explore natural areas, attend seminars, talk to experts, and visit with fellow natural landscapers, always keep a notebook handy to jot down anything that you want to look into further or keep in mind when designing your own landscape. For easier reference, you can organize the notebook into sections. One section might be devoted to attractive plant combinations, others to flowering times, site preparation, or maintenance. In this notebook, you can also record the dates and locations of places visited, tasks accomplished, and lists of plants purchased (and the source). A well-kept and organized notebook is a terrific asset.

In addition to taking notes, it's a good idea to take along a camera to keep a visual record of what you see. These photos can be used later for plant identification; to remind you of what an area looked like in early spring, midsummer, or fall; and to record the progress of your own landscape. If kept in an album with short, informative notes explaining each image, these photographs can become a valuable resource, something that can be shared with others wanting to learn from your personal experience.

Evaluating Your Site Conditions

As you look at the entire area surrounding your home and try to decide what you want or need to do, it is helpful to start with a site analysis of your yard. A site analysis is simply the process of making observations of and noting conditions in your yard and adjacent properties that might affect plant choice and positioning.

The first step in doing a site analysis is to get a measured drawing of your yard. Probably the easiest way to get one is to visit your town hall and request an aerial photograph of your property; this photograph, overlaid with lot lines, is usually on hand for property tax purposes. You can also print free aerial photographs off the Internet from such sites as **www.teraserver.com** or **mapquest.com,** but they will not have measured lot lines.

Enlarge the aerial photograph on a photocopier so that as you walk around your home you can make notes on the copy. Mark such features as areas that receive hot afternoon sun and are in need of a shade tree or a small grove of trees; note areas that receive morning sun, where less drought-tolerant plants would be more suitably located; and highlight overhead utility wires as an area to keep free of shade trees. Mark where windows and doors are located as areas of low or no vegetation. Draw arrows from windows where good landscaping would be most appreciated from inside your home. Highlight such things as parking areas to screen from view, a patio to keep more private, utility areas (with items such as the clothesline or air-conditioner unit) that may dictate plant choices—including areas that should be devoted to lawn. When all these elements are noted and taken into account, you can better determine where your priority areas are and how much your budget allows you to do in your first phase of landscaping. But you are not finished with your site analysis yet. Having considered aboveground factors that determine your plant selection and locations, you next need to look at your soil.

Taking a Look at Your Soil

Soil conditions are often responsible for a plant's thriving or failing in a given location. Therefore, an important consideration before deciding what you want to plant, and where you want to plant it, is determining the existing soil conditions in your yard. A soil's drainage rate, pH, fertility, and texture are all important factors in determining what plants will grow well in your home landscape. Observation of existing plants around your home or simple tests can determine all these factors.

SOIL DRAINAGE AND FERTILITY

Lawn and weeds already growing in your yard can be good indicators of soil drainage and fertility. Lawn does not grow on poorly drained soil, and it grows in excessively well-drained soil only if it is irrigated. A good stand of turfgrass is an indication that the soil in which it is growing is well drained and uncompacted. On the other hand, the presence of sedges and smartweed is a sign that the soil is poorly drained. Weeds such as chickweed, henbit, and lamb's-quarters are good indicators of soil fertile enough to support whatever native you might want to plant. Around new houses, where no turf or weeds are present to give clues about soil fertility and drainage, it is unknown whether the soil on the site can support vigorous plant growth. The soil may have been compacted by heavy machinery, which impedes drainage and limits root growth; or what was spread around your home could be sterile subsoil, which does not support plant growth at all. If these conditions exist, you must deal with them before you start planting. You can determine your soil's drainage and its fertility by the following methods:

Checking soil drainage To check how well your soil drains, dig several holes about a foot deep throughout your yard. Fill each hole to the top with water and observe how long the water stays in the hole. How quickly it drains depends on several factors, such as soil composition, time of year, and the amount of moisture already in the soil. If the water level drops less than one inch per hour, it may indicate that the soil is compacted or, at the very least, that it is poorly drained. If the soil is compacted, corrective actions such as deep tilling may be needed to improve drainage. In a soil that is well drained, the water should go down at a rate of 3 to 6 inches per hour. For an accurate reading, repeat the test until the rate of drainage is consistent.

Checking soil fertility Checking the fertility of the soil around a new house is also easy to do. One method is to ask your local Extension office where you can take a soil sample to be tested for nutrient deficiencies. What you get back from the testing facility is a printout of your soil's nutrient levels, an explanation of these numbers, and recommendations for correcting any nutrient deficiencies that might be found. Or you could simply observe how quickly weeds take over in your barren yard. If the weed growth is quick and lush, your transplants should also do fine. You may need to use a water sprinkler for this method to work if the weather does not cooperate. In addition, you could plant some radish seeds in your new yard. How well these fast-growing plants do gives you a good indication of how fertile your soil is. If they fail to thrive, you may be dealing with sterile subsoil rather than rich topsoil.

SOIL TEXTURE

The texture of a soil and its associated qualities are determined by the amount of clay, silt, and sand in the soil. Knowing the texture of your soil can help you determine what kind of plants will do well in your yard—or why something you planted was unsuccessful. Most plants are widely adaptable to a range of soil types, but plants do favor and even become genetically adapted to regional soil differences. For example, Butterfly Milkweed can grow in clay or sandy soil, but a particular strain of Butterfly Milkweed that has the ability to grow in sandy soil may not (probably *will* not) grow well in clay soil and vice versa. Also, knowing your soil texture allows a better understanding of its fertility, its tendency to become compacted, and its ability to hold and release moisture to plants.

Soils with a predominance of sand are loose and very well aerated but low in organic matter and therefore do not hold water or nutrients well. Compaction, however, is not a problem; and because these soils dry out so quickly, they can be worked earlier in the spring than moisture-retentive clay or silty soils. Silty soils tend to be poorly drained but high in nutrients; this tendency is due to the small size of a silt particle, up to one thousand times smaller than sand. These fertile soils are easily compacted when moist, and surface crusting is common after heavy rains. And as with silt, clay adds to a soil's tendency to be poorly drained and prone to compaction. The extremely fine, flat clay particles hold water tenaciously, causing soils with a predominance of clay to swell when wet, have a greasy feel when squeezed, and reveal a cracked and deeply fissured surface when dry. Poorly drained clay soils, however, are rich in nutrients and therefore more fertile than sandy soils.

You can determine the texture of your soil by a simple but accurate process done at home. Fill a clear, quart-size, glass jar one-third full with soil from your yard. (For a more accurate analysis, set up separate jars, with samples taken at different depths and locations throughout your yard.) After adding the soil and breaking up any large clods, fill the jar with water to within 2 inches of the top. Screw on the lid and shake the jar vigorously until all of the soil is suspended in the water. At this point, set the jar where it can sit undisturbed for at least 24 hours and where you can observe what is going on inside of the jar without moving it.

It will take just one minute for the relatively large and heavy sand particles to settle to the

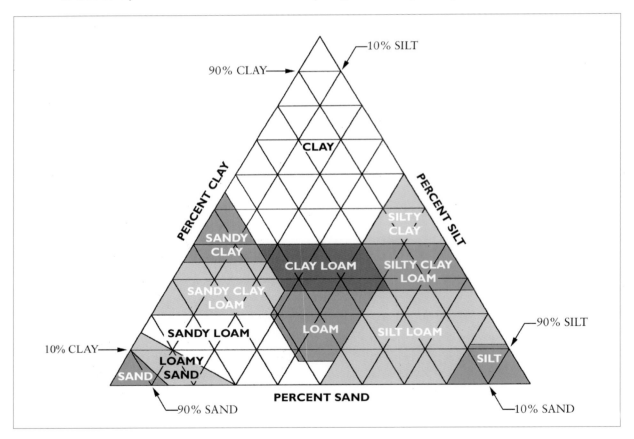

FIGURE 3.1 SOIL-TEXTURE TRIANGLE

NATIVE PLANTS IN THE HOME LANDSCAPE

bottom of the jar. Mark the level of sand on the jar at this time. The silt particles fall out of suspension 1 or 2 hours after the sand. While the sand layer is visibly gritty, the silt layer is dark, with no signs of grittiness. Mark the silt layer after 2 hours, but be careful not to include the thin layer of light-colored clay that might be suspended just above it. After 1 or 2 days, the clay settles and the water is clear; mark the layer of clay at this time. Determine the percentage of clay, silt, and sand in the jar from the measured thickness of each layer, divided by the total thickness of all three layers. Your soil type can then be found by using the soil-texture triangle (see figure 3.1). Where the percentage lines cross one another is your exact soil type.

SOIL PH

Soil reaction, or pH, is a measurement of acidity or alkalinity. Knowing the pH of your soil—that is, whether it is acidic, neutral, or alkaline—is important because it determines what nutrients will be available to your plants and therefore what plants will do well at various pH levels. For example, if your soil is acidic, the essential nutrient phosphorus may be unavailable to your plants in the quantities that they need. If it is alkaline, nutrients such as iron, boron, copper, and zinc—all vital in minor amounts for most plants to thrive—are locked up in your soil and unavailable to your plants.

The pH scale ranges from 1.0 (acidic) to 14.0 (alkaline), with 7.0 being a neutral reading. The pH scale is logarithmic, which means that a soil with a pH of 5.0 is 10 times more acidic than a soil with a pH of 6.0 and 100 times more acidic than a soil with a pH of 7.0. Some plants do well only in soils that are acidic, others in alkaline; but most plants thrive where the soil is slightly acidic to neutral (between 5.8 and 7.2). In this range, essential plant nutrients are most available to the plants.

Testing the pH of a soil is not something that you need to do every time you want to plant something. But you should have the soil around your home tested at least once so that you know the relative acidity or alkalinity of your soil. This information helps you in determining which plants might do well and which ones might prove to be disappointments. There are many kits and various apparatuses available at garden centers for testing soil pH, or you can call your local Extension office to find out where you can take a sample of your soil to be tested.

TOP: FRUIT OF THE WINTERBERRY HOLLY SHRUB (*Ilex verticillata*)

MIDDLE: FLOWERS OF THE THORNLESS COCKSPUR HAWTHORN (*Crataegus crusgalli* var. *inermis*)

BOTTOM: WOODLAND SUNFLOWER (*Helianthus strumosus*)

CHAPTER FOUR

Plants of the Tallgrass Region

THE PLANTS FOR THIS BOOK were chosen for their commercial availability, visual attractiveness, multiple seasons of interest, ease of culture, and suitability to a small site. They are listed alphabetically under each heading by their botanical, or latinized, names; alternative or older botanical names sometimes found in field guides or catalogs are listed in brackets.

Of the hundreds of plants native to the upper Midwest, many are not good choices for the typical small yard. Some, such as Cup Plant or New England Aster, are easily grown but get too large and overwhelming in a small space. Some plants may be too aggressive, as with many of the goldenrods, quickly crowding out other plants and becoming a maintenance headache. Others may be better suited to wild areas due to their weedy appearance when used in the home landscape. Still others may be unsuitable for most designed landscapes due to their slow growth or special requirements, such as consistent soil moisture or sandy soils. The plants selected for this book, if properly situated, are all easily maintained and appropriate for the well-designed front yard landscape. There is no need to hide these great plants in the backyard: Their beauty is unsurpassed.

What's in a Name?

Knowing the botanical name of a plant is important when searching for information about it in a reference book or even when looking for a certain plant to purchase from a nursery catalog. Botanical names, such as *Podophyllum peltatum*, are specific; they refer to only one plant. Common names, Mayapple in this case, are sometimes used for more than one species of plant; or a plant may have several common names associated with it. To avoid confusion, always try to learn the botanical names, along with the common names, of the plants that you are interested in. The names may at first seem as difficult to pronounce as to remember, but no more so than the names of your friends and coworkers; just think of the plants as friends with exotic-sounding names.

A botanical name should always be underlined or italicized and is composed of two parts, the genus (generic name) and the specific epithet. Together, these two components refer to a particular species of plant. The genus, in this case *Podophyllum* (meaning stalked leaf), is always capitalized and groups together a set of plants that have certain similarities. If the genus is understood in a text passage, it may be abbreviated to one letter followed by the specific epithet. The specific epithet, which is not capitalized, describes a particular species; for example, *peltatum* indicates a plant with leaves that resemble a small, leather shield, or pelta, used by the Roman army.

You may, in addition to the genus and specific epithet, see variety or cultivar names attached to some plants, such as *Crataegus crusgalli* var. *inermis* or *Rhus typhina* 'Laciniata'. A variety, preceded by "var." and italicized, is distinguished from the straight species by having certain inheritable traits, in this case thornlessness. A cultivar (cultivated variety) name, by contrast, is capitalized and indicated by single quotation marks. Cultivars also have characteristics that differ from the straight species; but these traits are not passed on genetically through seeds, and hence these plants must be reproduced by root or stem cuttings.

WILDFLOWERS

COMMON NAME	**NODDING ONION**
BOTANICAL NAME	*Allium cernuum*
Height	12"
Spread	12"
Bloom time	Mid- to late summer
Flower	1½", white to pink cluster
Exposure	Sun to partial shade
Soil moisture	Dry to mesic
Spacing	12"

Nodding Onion is inconspicuous in the landscape until it comes into flower in midsummer. At that time, the buds slowly unfurl to form a small ball of star-shaped flowers on foot-tall stems. Planted along the outside edge of taller wildflowers such as Pale Purple Coneflower and Foxglove Beard Tongue, it puts on a stunning show. The clumps of flat, grasslike leaves are attractive throughout the growing season and look good growing among the coarse-leafed Stiff Goldenrod and Prairie Dock.

CULTURE Nodding Onion is found growing in mesic and dry prairies and on the sandy shores of Lake Michigan. It grows in most settings, sun or shade, moist or dry; but it does best in a sunny, well-drained site. If planted in poorly drained soil, its roots may rot. It spreads by seed and bulb offshoots.

COMMON NAME	CHICAGOUA
BOTANICAL NAME	*Allium tricoccum*
Height	10"
Spread	4"
Bloom time	Early summer
Flower	1", white ball
Exposure	Partial shade to shade
Soil moisture	Mesic
Spacing	12"

Chicagoua is the Algonquin Indian word for this plant. Early inhabitants of the southwestern shore of Lake Michigan found it growing in such abundance that they eventually referred to this region as "Chicago," in reference to this woodland leek.

Chicagoua can be found growing in woodlands with rich, sandy soil. It is an interesting plant in that it sends up leaves, somewhat resembling Lily-of-the-Valley but with a purple tint to them, in early spring. The leaves die back and disappear by early summer. When they are gone, the plant sends up multiple, 8-inch stalks, each topped by a ball of small, star-shaped, white flowers—a real surprise and very showy.

CULTURE Chicagoua prefers moist, rich, well-drained soil, where it spreads to form colonies but is not invasive. In average, more droughty garden soil, the plant forms small, one-foot-wide clumps. The bulbs of this plant, which are edible, should be planted just below the surface of the soil. Chicagoua is great for bringing interest to the shade garden when few other woodland plants are in flower.

COMMON NAME	COLUMBINE
BOTANICAL NAME	*Aquilegia canadensis*
Height	18"
Spread	18"
Bloom time	Mid- to late spring
Flower	1 1/2", scarlet with yellow
Exposure	Partial shade to sun
Soil moisture	Mesic
Spacing	12"

Found in a diverse range of habitats, including mesic woods, Black Oak savannas, and calcareous fens, Columbine does well in the shade garden. From mid- to late spring, the plants are covered by flowers of scarlet and yellow that defy simple description but are quite showy; and hummingbirds seem to enjoy their nectar. Columbine is an attractive plant even out of flower, with its horizontal tiers of delicate blue–green foliage. Once established, this plant freely self-sows throughout the garden and should be pulled as necessary so as not to compete with other wildflowers for space.

CULTURE Columbine does well in shade or full sun but does best and is most appreciated when grown in the shade garden. It may become overgrown if planted in rich, moist soil, forming more compact plants in poor, gravelly soil. This plant forms a deep taproot that allows it to tolerate dry shade, but it suffers in poorly drained clay soils.

COMMON NAME	JACK-IN-THE-PULPIT
BOTANICAL NAME	*Arisaema triphyllum [A. atrorubens]*
Height	12–18" (up to 3')
Spread	8–12"
Bloom time	Midspring
Flower	2", green with purple
Exposure	Full to partial shade
Soil moisture	Mesic
Spacing	Random

Jack-in-the-Pulpit is one of our most exotic-looking woodland plants. Like its relative the Calla Lily, it grows from a bulbous corm, but the resemblance ends there. It has a large, three-parted leaf that shelters an unusual, hooded flower consisting of "Jack" (a one-inch-long cylinder, or spadix, with inconspicuous male and/or female flowers at its base) and a green hood, or spathe, with a purple-striped interior that encloses Jack and forms his bully pulpit. After flowering, the mature plant produces a 2-inch seed cluster resembling a green raspberry, which turns bright red in fall. Jack makes a good specimen plant throughout the shade garden.

CULTURE Jack-in-the-Pulpit enjoys a moist, rich soil and can grow to 3 feet. However, it also does well and is often found growing in dry woods, reaching a height of one foot. Easy to grow, it eventually forms small colonies, as the fallen seeds germinate readily. Young plants produce only male flowers, thus no seed heads; and their leaves tend to be more ephemeral, withering more quickly than those of mature, fruit-producing plants. Plant corms 3 to 4 inches deep.

COMMON NAME	WOODLAND GINGER
BOTANICAL NAME	*Asarum canadense*
Height	6"
Spread	Colonies
Bloom time	Midspring
Flower	$^5/_8$", urn-shaped, maroon
Exposure	Full to partial shade
Soil moisture	Mesic
Spacing	8"

Woodland Ginger, found in flood plain and upland woods, forms a green carpet of 3-inch, kidney-shaped leaves that look good all season. Although it's not a true ginger, its leaves, when picked, smell like the tropical, culinary ginger *(Zingiber officinale)*. Its bold leaves complement the finely cut leaves of Maidenhair Fern and Christmas Fern, as well as the taller Columbine and Woodland Geranium. Woodland Ginger's flowers, which are not showy, are hidden beneath its leaves. Given time and rich soil, this plant forms a solid groundcover and should be encouraged and given the space to do so.

CULTURE Woodland Ginger is carefree and easy to grow in mesic, well-drained garden soil. It may need supplemental watering if the soil becomes dry for an extended period in midsummer; it appreciates a 2-inch layer of shredded-leaf mulch to conserve moisture. Woodland Ginger is easily transplanted and spreads by horizontal stems that lie at or just below the surface.

NATIVE PLANTS IN THE HOME LANDSCAPE

COMMON NAME	**BUTTERFLY MILKWEED**
BOTANICAL NAME	*Asclepias tuberosa*
Height	18–24"
Spread	18"
Bloom time	Early summer
Flower	2", orange cluster
Exposure	Full sun to partial shade
Soil moisture	Dry to mesic
Spacing	18"

No garden should be without this long-lived, easy-to-grow perennial. It forms a compact plant with attractive foliage all season and spectacular orange flowers in early summer. Although often found growing in sandy savanna soils, it tolerates a wide range of soil conditions, including clay. Butterflies, such as monarchs, fritillaries, and coral hairstreaks, are attracted to the nectar of the flowers; the foliage provides food for queens and monarch caterpillars.

CULTURE Butterfly Milkweed prefers a well-drained soil and performs best if placed where it receives plenty of sun. The deep, coarse root system makes this plant difficult to move once established; but these roots also make the plant very drought-tolerant. This plant thrives with little attention once established. In fact, if given too much water, the roots are prone to rot; for this reason, mulching is not recommended. Mark the location of this slow-to-emerge plant to avoid disturbing its shoots that lie just below the surface of the soil in late spring.

COMMON NAME	**AROMATIC ASTER**
BOTANICAL NAME	*Aster oblongifolius*
Height	24"
Spread	18"
Bloom time	Early to midfall
Flower	1", pale blue head
Exposure	Full sun
Soil moisture	Dry to mesic
Spacing	12"

A truly midwestern aster, Aromatic Aster is found growing on limestone barrens from Minnesota to Texas. Similar in flower to the New England Aster *(Aster novae-angliae)*, this butterfly magnet is often one of the last plants of the season to bloom. The patient gardener is rewarded with a spectacular show of purple flowers, sometimes touched with morning frost. Rarely growing taller than 2 feet, this plant does not overpower its companions in a small landscape garden, as often is the case with the much taller New England Aster.

CULTURE Once established, this plant thrives with benign neglect and is quite drought-tolerant. Place this aster in sites too dry for New England Aster, which prefers a more consistently moist soil. Also, unlike the 5- to 6-foot-tall New England Aster, Aromatic Aster is not prone to flop over in flower if not supported by staking. This elegant, underutilized aster deserves a place in the home landscape.

COMMON NAME	**WHITE PRAIRIE INDIGO**
BOTANICAL NAME	*Baptisia leucantha [B. lactea]*
Height	36"
Spread	3–5'
Bloom time	Late spring
Flower	12", white raceme
Exposure	Sun to partial shade
Soil moisture	Dry to mesic
Spacing	36"

White Prairie Indigo emerges from the ground in late spring like a stalk of asparagus, its racemes of white, pea-like flowers appearing atop the 2-foot-tall stem just as the leaves begin to unfurl to produce an umbrella-like canopy up to 5 feet across. Although the hummingbird-attracting flowers are present for only a week, this unusual plant has attractive, blue–green foliage throughout the growing season. Underplant with shorter wildflowers and grasses; keep taller plants at least 3 feet away to allow for White Prairie Indigo's canopy of growth.

CULTURE This nitrogen-fixing legume is best used as a specimen plant due to its curious growth habit. Place this plant in sun or partial shade. It is tolerant of a wide range of soils from moist to moderately dry although it flowers best on dry sites. The coarse root system can grow down 10 feet, making this plant drought-tolerant and carefree.

COMMON NAME	**CREAM PRAIRIE INDIGO**
BOTANICAL NAME	*Baptisia leucophaea [B. bracteata]*
Height	12"
Spread	24–30"
Bloom time	Midspring
Flower	8", pendulous, pale yellow raceme
Exposure	Sun to partial shade
Soil moisture	Dry to mesic
Spacing	24"

Cream Prairie Indigo is much shorter than White Prairie Indigo; and its large, pendulous, pale yellow flowers appear a week or so earlier. Slow-growing and long-lived, it forms a small, shrublike plant 2 feet across and a foot or so tall. The compact habit, early season of bloom, and attractive, weeping foliage throughout the season make it a great foreground plant for the home landscape. A blue dye can be produced from this plant by steeping the foliage in hot water and then allowing the mixture to ferment.

CULTURE Site this plant, which can be found growing in dry and mesic prairies and open woodlands, under similar conditions as White Prairie Indigo. Cream Prairie Indigo prefers full sun but does well in partial shade and in a wide range of soils. Baptisias are slow to mature.

COMMON NAME	**SPRING BEAUTY**
BOTANICAL NAME	*Claytonia virginica*
Height	4–6"
Spread	2"
Bloom time	Early spring
Flower	¹/₄", 5-petaled, pink
Exposure	Partial shade to full sun
Soil moisture	Mesic
Spacing	Random

Spring Beauty is a small plant but occurs in such great numbers that it forms a sea of small, pink flowers across the woodland floor—a spectacular sight. The small clusters of flowers welcome the early spring sun, following its movement throughout the day and refusing to open, lacking its direction, on overcast days. It is tough enough to grow in lawns but is killed by "weed-and-feed" fertilizers. Plant the small, bulbous corms throughout your yard, both in sun and shade. Over the years, they multiply and reward you with a show every spring, disappearing without a trace by the middle of June.
CULTURE Spring Beauty does well in most well-drained soils. Plant corms randomly throughout the garden about 3 inches deep. Plants emerge early, enjoying spring moisture, and go dormant by the start of summer's heat.

COMMON NAME	**PALE PURPLE CONEFLOWER**
BOTANICAL NAME	*Echinacea pallida*
Height	2–3'
Spread	8"
Bloom time	Early to midsummer
Flower	2", rosey pink head
Exposure	Full sun
Soil moisture	Dry to mesic
Spacing	8"

Often overlooked in favor of Purple Coneflower *(Echinacea purpurea)*, Pale Purple Coneflower is better suited to the dry, sunny garden. Pale Purple Coneflower has a deep taproot that allows it to tolerate droughty conditions better than the fibrous root system of the Purple Coneflower, whose natural habitat is the more moist and shady oak savanna. Pale Purple Coneflower blooms earlier, occurring in early summer when few other sun-loving plants are in flower; Purple Coneflower blooms in later midsummer. Pale Purple Coneflower's narrow leaves allow it to be easily mixed with other plants without losing any flower power. In fact, when it is interplanted with Little Bluestem, Flowering Spurge, Yellow Coneflower, Purple Prairie Clover, and Aromatic Aster, a continuous show of color and an extended season of interest can be achieved in a small space.

Besides their beauty, coneflowers provide nectar for hummingbirds and butterflies; the leaves provide food for the Ottoe skipper larva.
CULTURE Plant Pale Purple Coneflower in well-drained soil in direct sunlight. Once established, Pale Purple Coneflower can be difficult to move due to its taproot. If left alone, it does well with little care. Coneflowers generally resent soil kept excessively moist by irrigation or poor drainage: The plants fail to thrive, and root rot may occur.

COMMON NAME	RATTLESNAKE MASTER
BOTANICAL NAME	*Eryngium yuccifolium*
Height	18–24"
Spread	18"
Bloom time	Midsummer
Flower	$^3/_4$", gray–green ball
Exposure	Full sun
Soil moisture	Dry to mesic
Spacing	10"

In leaf, the blue–gray, saberlike leaves of Rattlesnake Master resemble those of the Yucca plant, hence its specific epithet *yuccifolium;* but in flower, there is no confusing the two. In midsummer, Rattlesnake Master sends up a single stem that rises 3 feet, topped by head-turning flowers in the form of $^3/_4$-inch, spiky balls. The nectar attracts butterflies and bees. The unique form and gray color of this plant, good throughout the growing season, complement its companions and make it a must in the home landscape. CULTURE This long-lived plant demands full sun and well-drained soil but does equally well in nutrient-poor, sandy or clay soil. Once established, Rattlesnake Master does not like to be moved. Use the dramatic foliage to its best advantage by placing Rattlesnake Master in the foreground of the landscape in groups of three. It is nice in front of other, taller plants, such as Yellow Coneflower and Indiangrass, with Pasture Rose and Waukegan Creeping Juniper at its base.

COMMON NAME	WHITE TROUT LILY
BOTANICAL NAME	*Erythronium albidum*
Height	4"
Spread	2"
Bloom time	Early spring
Flower	1", trumpet-shaped, white
Exposure	Partial shade
Soil moisture	Mesic
Spacing	6"

White Trout Lily rises, blooms, and disappears all within a month's time. Found growing in wooded bottomlands and ravines, it freely self-sows to form a solid groundcover of 4-inch, tuliplike, gray–green and purple-mottled leaves, with two leaves arising from each underground corm. A small, white flower resembling a miniature Day Lily hangs at the end of a 6-inch stem, a display that is outdone by the rich color of the leaves. Plant this spring ephemeral throughout the shade garden, allowing it to colonize large areas. It flowers at the same time as Virginia Bluebells.
CULTURE White Trout Lily does best in rich, moist, well-drained sites but tolerates drier sites than the very similar Yellow Trout Lily *(Erythronium americanum),* which occurs less commonly in the Midwest but is more readily available commercially. Both appreciate a 2-inch layer of shredded-leaf mulch. Plant corms about 3 inches deep.

NATIVE PLANTS IN THE HOME LANDSCAPE

COMMON NAME	FLOWERING SPURGE
BOTANICAL NAME	*Euphorbia corollata*
Height	12–36"
Spread	8–12"
Bloom time	Early to late summer
Flower	6–12", white spray
Exposure	Sun to partial shade
Soil moisture	Dry to mesic
Spacing	8–12"

Do not let the delicate, mistlike flowers of Flowering Spurge fool you. This inhabitant of the high dunes and other dry places takes harsh conditions in stride, including heat, cold, and wind. Blooming for most of the growing season, this plant—with its 18-inch, unbranched stems, topped by a cloud of $^1/_8$-inch, white blossoms—works well in combination with most other prairie grasses and wildflowers. Used as a cut flower, it enhances any arrangement.
CULTURE Flowering Spurge seems to thrive in hot, dry sites. Not at all fussy, it has a deep taproot that allows it to take hold and grow with little attention from the gardener. Place it in full sun or filtered shade; it is adaptable to sandy or clay soils, average moisture to drought conditions. Its single, upright stem allows it to be interplanted gracefully with such companions as Yellow Coneflower, Little Bluestem, Purple Prairie Clover, and Blazing Star. It is a must for any prairie garden.

COMMON NAME	SCARLET STRAWBERRY
BOTANICAL NAME	*Fragaria virginiana*
Height	6–12"
Spread	6–10"
Bloom time	Midspring
Flower	$^5/_8$", 5-petaled, white
Exposure	Sun to partial shade
Soil moisture	Mesic
Spacing	8"

Not often thought of as ornamental, Scarlet Strawberry is actually a great plant for the home landscape. Low-growing, with delicate, white flowers in midspring and attractive, three-parted leaves all season long, this plant makes a good groundcover along woodland edges, around and among a patch of Gray Dogwood, or interplanted with other, much taller wildflowers for an added dimension. The tasty fruit is an additional benefit to both wildlife and the family.
CULTURE Occurring in a wide variety of habitats, strawberries are not at all fussy about where they grow. Plant in full sun or under and among deciduous trees and shrubs, where they appreciate the added shade in midsummer. With its attractive foliage all season, Scarlet Strawberry is an excellent accent plant to use throughout the landscape as a unifying element. Do not plant Scarlet Strawberry where its tendency to spread becomes a maintenance problem.

COMMON NAME	WOODLAND GERANIUM
BOTANICAL NAME	*Geranium maculatum*
Height	12"
Spread	12"
Bloom time	Midspring to early summer
Flower	2", 5-petaled, pink
Exposure	Partial shade to sun
Soil moisture	Mesic
Spacing	12"

Woodland Geranium is a common forest and savanna wildflower with an extended season of bloom and attractive mounds of coarsely toothed foliage throughout the growing season. As the seed capsules mature, they spring open, shooting seeds far and wide throughout the garden, establishing seedlings some distance from the parent plant. Woodland Geranium is good in moderation but needs to be kept from overtaking and outcompeting less aggressive woodland plants. It looks good with Woodland Ginger in the foreground and Columbine behind.

CULTURE This plant does well in most shaded settings or, if kept moist, in full sun. It may wither or go dormant in extended drought and therefore may need supplemental watering to stay green. Mulching with 2 inches of shredded leaves helps conserve soil moisture. Cutting back faded flowers encourages an extended bloom time.

COMMON NAME	PRAIRIE SMOKE
BOTANICAL NAME	*Geum triflorum*
Height	6"
Spread	8"
Bloom time	Mid- to late spring
Flower	1", drooping, dark red head
Exposure	Sun to partial shade
Soil moisture	Dry to mesic
Spacing	8"

Found in dry woods and prairies, Prairie Smoke gets its name from the smokelike, wispy seed structures that appear after the inconspicuous, deep red flowers finish blooming in mid- to late spring. A low-growing plant, it forms a solid mat of groundcover if given the chance. It looks best planted as a foreground plant in masses covering 3 to 4 square feet.

CULTURE For best success, give this plant a sunny site with well-drained soil. It prefers an alkaline soil and may benefit by digging in crushed limestone at the time of planting. This plant slowly spreads by sending out side shoots but can be kept in check with a sharp hoe, or its offspring can be transplanted easily to other parts of the garden.

COMMON NAME	**WOODLAND SUNFLOWER**
BOTANICAL NAME	*Helianthus strumosus*
Height	24"
Spread	Colonies
Bloom time	Mid- to late summer
Flower	2", yellow head
Exposure	Sun to partial shade
Soil moisture	Dry to mesic
Spacing	8"

Often found along the edges of oak woods, this is one sunflower that does not mind a little shade—in fact, it welcomes it. Growing to a height of only 2 feet, Woodland Sunflower is covered with 2-inch, bright yellow blossoms from mid- to late summer and has nice, clean foliage all season. It is perfect for brightening up a part of the landscape that receives sun for only part of the day.

CULTURE Naturally occurring in dry clay in full sun as well as in rich forest soil under oaks, Woodland Sunflower adapts to most growing situations. Best when used in sweeping masses, it naturally spreads to form large colonies and should be placed in an area where this can occur. Mature plants are easily moved in springtime.

COMMON NAME	**SHARP-LOBED HEPATICA**
BOTANICAL NAME	*Hepatica acutiloba*
Height	6"
Spread	10"
Bloom time	Early spring
Flower	$^3/_4$", 6-sepaled, white or violet
Exposure	Partial to full shade
Soil moisture	Dry to mesic
Spacing	10"

There may be other woodland wildflowers as beautiful but none more beautiful than Sharp-lobed Hepatica. Just as the last of winter's flakes are falling, hepatica is sending up clusters of 3-inch-tall flower stalks, forming little bouquets of bloom. After the blooms begin to fade, gossamer, three-lobed leaves appear, forming tight mounds of foliage that look good all season, even sticking around through winter, although turning a little purple in the brisk air. Hepatica looks especially nice planted in groups of three or five near a path where the delicate-looking plants and flowers can be appreciated.

CULTURE Often found on shaded slopes in dry and mesic woods, hepatica does well in dry to moist, well-drained soils with average richness. Leaves brown if the plant receives too much direct sun. This plant demands little but has a great deal to offer.

COMMON NAME	**PRAIRIE ALUMROOT**
BOTANICAL NAME	*Heuchera richardsonii*
Height	8–12"
Spread	12"
Bloom time	Late spring to late summer
Flower	$^{1}/_{4}$", bell-shaped, green
Exposure	Sun to partial shade
Soil moisture	Dry to wet
Spacing	12"

Better appreciated for its attractive, rounded foliage with filigree edges and mounded habit than for its spikes of $^{1}/_{4}$-inch, greenish white flowers, Prairie Alumroot looks best when massed in front of taller wildflowers or, if more formality is desired, as a border along the edge of a planting bed.
CULTURE Naturally occurring in dry, wet, and mesic prairies, as well as open woods, this carefree plant thrives in most settings but especially in rich, well-drained soils. In shade, the plant is less compact and has a more open habit. You may need to divide it every 3 years or so, as an older plant's sprawling stems tend to leave the center of the plant leafless and less attractive.

BLAZING STAR

More than 40 species of blazing star occur in North America. Most do best in soils with consistent moisture, but some prefer the dry conditions found in many home landscapes. Two of the blazing stars mentioned here do well in dry sites: Rough Blazing Star and Dwarf Blazing Star. Prairie Blazing Star prefers a more consistently moist soil. All have beautiful, deep pink flowers in late summer and narrow, moisture-conserving leaves along an unbranched stem. Butterflies, hummingbirds, and bees are attracted to the flowers, which are great dried or fresh in flower arrangements; and finches relish the seeds.

COMMON NAME	**ROUGH BLAZING STAR**
BOTANICAL NAME	*Liatris aspera*
Height	2–5"
Spread	10"
Bloom time	Mid- to late summer
Flower	Tufted, 10", pink spike (occasionally white)
Exposure	Sun to partial sun
Soil moisture	Dry to mesic
Spacing	8–12"

Found in dry prairies and sandy savannas, this blazing star forms an attractive plant 2 to 3 feet tall when placed in a dry, sunny, well-drained site. In partial shade, the stems reach for the sun, losing their vertical character. Individual tufts of small, pink flowers form a foot-long spike at the end of a 4-foot stem. Each plant can potentially form several stems. This plant is a star among the late-season bloomers. In moist, fertile soil, the stems grow taller and must be supported by staking.

COMMON NAME	DWARF BLAZING STAR
BOTANICAL NAME	*Liatris cylindracea*
Height	12–18"
Spread	12"
Bloom time	Mid- to late summer
Flower	2–4", pink cluster
Exposure	Sun
Soil moisture	Dry
Spacing	10"

As does Rough Blazing Star, Dwarf Blazing Star prefers a dry, sunny, well-drained location, but it grows to only 18 inches tall. This plant, with unbranched stems and narrow leaves up to 10 inches long, can be found growing along the sandy shore of Lake Michigan and inland on dry prairies. This compact plant produces short clusters of pink flowers and looks great in the foreground along with Waukegan Creeping Juniper.

COMMON NAME	PRAIRIE BLAZING STAR
BOTANICAL NAME	*Liatris pycnostachya*
Height	2–5'
Spread	10"
Bloom time	Late summer
Flower	Dense, 10", pink spike
Exposure	Full sun
Soil moisture	Mesic to moist
Spacing	8–12"

Similar to Rough Blazing Star, Prairie Blazing Star can send up unbranched stems 5 feet tall; but rather than a tufted flower spike, it forms a solid, narrow spike of pink flowers, which appear just before those of Rough Blazing Star. Also, unlike the other two blazing stars mentioned, Prairie Blazing Star prefers a soil that is more consistently moist. The long stems may require staking or planting among other wildflowers for support.

COMMON NAME	**GREAT BLUE LOBELIA**
BOTANICAL NAME	*Lobelia siphilitica*
Height	1–3'
Spread	12–18"
Bloom time	Late summer to early fall
Flower	4–6", blue spike
Exposure	Sun to partial shade
Soil moisture	Mesic to wet
Spacing	12"

Found growing in wooded floodplains and around sunny pond edges, Great Blue Lobelia has erect, unbranched stems topped by spikes of 4- to 6-inch, bright sky blue flowers toward the end of the growing season, making this plant especially nice in the shade garden when few others are in bloom. Great Blue Lobelia is best when massed or planted in groups of three throughout the shaded landscape.

CULTURE Great Blue Lobelia—although normally found growing near streams and ponds (where constant moisture is available) and attaining heights of 3 feet or more—is quite tough and adaptable to average garden conditions. In partly shady locations, it does well in sandy or clay soils, staying more compact, at about one foot in height with average soil moisture. In most home landscapes, this plant benefits if the soil is enriched with compost and mulched with 2 inches of shredded leaves. In full sun, supplemental watering is necessary if the soil becomes dry.

CARDINAL FLOWER, *Lobelia cardinalis*

Cardinal Flower is similar in habit and culture to Great Blue Lobelia but has stunning, scarlet red rather than blue flowers. Also, Cardinal Flower needs soil that is much more moist, and it is short-lived in sites lacking consistent soil moisture. It can be grown in full sun or partial shade and is otherwise a carefree and easy-to-grow plant. Lobelias generally do not do well in competition with other plants and, therefore, require their own space in the landscape.

COMMON NAME	VIRGINIA BLUEBELLS
BOTANICAL NAME	*Mertensia virginica*
Height	12"
Spread	12"
Bloom time	Early to midspring
Flower	1", bell-shapped, pale blue
Exposure	Partial shade
Soil moisture	Mesic to wet
Spacing	12"

Found blanketing wooded floodplains and putting on a spectacular show of blue flowers, Virginia Bluebells does very well in average to poor garden soil. It blooms at the same time as White Trout Lily, Woodland Phlox, Woodland Geranium, Smooth Solomon's Seal, and the trilliums. Plant it throughout the shade garden, but keep massings small so that it does not become distracting as the foliage yellows and flops over after flowering. Virginia Bluebells works best when planted at the base of trees and woodland shrubs, such as Downy Serviceberry and Blackhaw Viburnum, so that large voids are not noticed when plants go dormant. This plant is very nice in a grove of River Birch. The flowers attract hummingbirds and female bumblebees, the only bumblebees to fly in early spring.

CULTURE This plant thrives in average, well-drained soil, staying more compact in poorer soils. In rich soils, Virginia Bluebells can become an aggressive spreader and should be kept in check, especially in the small shade garden.

COMMON NAME	FOXGLOVE BEARD TONGUE
BOTANICAL NAME	*Penstemon digitalis*
Height	24"
Spread	12"
Bloom time	Late spring to early summer
Flower	6", white to pink raceme
Exposure	Sun to partial shade
Soil moisture	Dry to mesic
Spacing	10"

Hummingbirds are drawn to this plant's white flower spikes that appear in early summer just before many other wildflowers come into bloom. The flowers, leaves, and stems are tinged a pinkish red, providing added interest to the landscape. Attractive both in and out of flower, this plant has a vertical growth habit that allows it to be used effectively massed in groups of three to six plants; mixed among other species, such as Golden Alexanders or Spiderwort; and behind Blue-eyed Grass.

CULTURE This plant can grow and is found growing just about anywhere, including a crack in the sidewalk. It is naturally found in mesic woods and prairies. It is not invasive but also not fussy about where it grows. Plant in full sun or partial shade, in well-drained or poorly drained soil. It does best in full sun with average soil moisture. Its fibrous root system allows it to be divided and replanted with ease.

COMMON NAME	**PURPLE PRAIRIE CLOVER**
BOTANICAL NAME	*Petalostemum purpureum [Dalea purpurea]*
Height	12–24"
Spread	12"
Bloom time	Early to midsummer
Flower	2", rosy purple spike
Exposure	Sun to partial shade
Soil moisture	Dry to mesic
Spacing	12"

Blooming for up to 2 months atop 2-foot-tall, upright stems, Purple Prairie Clover is most effective in the landscape when interplanted with Penstemon, Little Bluestem, Scarlet Strawberry, and Aromatic Aster. It is also good interplanted with Golden Alexanders. This member of the pea family enriches the soil by pulling nitrogen from the air; this captured nitrogen enriches the soil and is ultimately used by other plants as well. The leaves of this plant are a food source for sulfur butterfly offspring. The little, thimblelike seed heads provide winter interest in the garden.

CULTURE This tough plant grows well in full sun to partial shade and is tolerant of a wide range of soils but prefers average to dry conditions. The taproot can reach depths of 5 feet. Purple Prairie Clover is drought-tolerant and carefree but difficult to move once established. Rabbits particularly enjoy browsing on this plant's foliage.

COMMON NAME	**WOODLAND PHLOX**
BOTANICAL NAME	*Phlox divaricata*
Height	12"
Spread	10"
Bloom time	Midspring
Flower	1", 5-petaled, pale blue
Exposure	Partial shade
Soil moisture	Mesic
Spacing	10"

Woodland Phlox puts on a nice show of pale blue flowers atop one-foot stems in midspring. Allow it to spread at will throughout the shade garden, removing only those plants that begin to compete visually with smaller, more delicate flowers such as trilliums and hepatica. Woodland Phlox looks good growing up through Woodland Ginger or sedges. Hummingbirds and butterflies are attracted to its flowers.

CULTURE Woodland Phlox prefers rich, moist soil but does well in average, well-drained soil with normal springtime precipitation. Its fibrous roots need dependable watering to become established in a new location. It is an undemanding plant that adds an understated beauty to the springtime shade garden.

COMMON NAME	MAYAPPLE
BOTANICAL NAME	*Podophyllum peltatum*
Height	12"
Spread	8–10"
Bloom time	Midspring
Flower	1", white-petaled
Exposure	Shade to partial sun
Soil moisture	Mesic
Spacing	10"

Everything about Mayapple is big and bold. Its leaves are as broad as an outstretched hand, and it forms colonies 6 feet or more across—not a plant for the faint of heart or for a shade garden with limited space. It can easily be kept from spreading but looks best when allowed to do so. The showy flowers are hidden beneath the foliage and are seldom noticed. Mayapple is good as a groundcover under Gray Dogwood and Blackhaw Viburnum, where it can spread with impunity.

CULTURE This carefree plant can be found growing in upland woods and oak openings. Arising in midspring from a rhizome just below the surface of the soil, it performs best in rich soil and partial shade but does well in most soils with good drainage, even in full sun. Dry soil in midsummer causes its leaves to turn yellow and go dormant until next spring. Mulch with 2 inches of shredded leaves to conserve soil moisture.

COMMON NAME	JACOB'S LADDER
BOTANICAL NAME	*Polemonium reptans*
Height	12"
Spread	12"
Bloom time	Midspring
Flower	1/2", bell-shaped, blue
Exposure	Partial to full shade
Soil moisture	Mesic
Spacing	10"

This easy-to-grow plant has leaves that are almost fernlike and form nice mounds of foliage covered with pale blue flowers in midspring. The ornamental foliage stays green and attractive throughout the growing season and looks good interplanted with other woodland wildflowers such as Jack-in-the-Pulpit, Chicagoua, Virginia Bluebells, Woodland Phlox, and Penn Sedge. The commonly available *P. caeruleum*, which grows to a height of 18 to 24 inches and is also known as Jacob's Ladder, is a native of northern European and western North American woods.

CULTURE In rich, moist soil, Jacob's Ladder may form a groundcover; but in average garden soil with good drainage, the plants form compact mounds of foliage. Either way, this plant is attractive both in and out of flower. Jacob's Ladder, which emerges in midspring from a shallow rhizome, appreciates additional water in extended dry periods; mulching with 2 inches of shredded leaves helps conserve soil moisture. Dividing this plant every 3 years or so increases its vigor and floral display.

COMMON NAME	**SMOOTH SOLOMON'S SEAL**
BOTANICAL NAME	*Polygonatum canaliculatum [P. biflorum, P. commutatum]*
Height	24"
Spread	24"
Bloom time	Mid- to late spring
Flower	$1/2$", bell-shaped, yellow
Exposure	Partial to full shade
Soil moisture	Dry to mesic
Spacing	Random

The arching, 1- to 3-foot stems of Smooth Solomon's Seal add interest to the shade garden throughout the growing season. Pendulous flowers hang from each leaf node—nice when backlit by the sun. In autumn, the half-inch, black berries contrast with the yellowing foliage. This plant looks good planted throughout the garden, especially at the base of trees.

CULTURE Not at all fussy about soil moisture or where it grows, Smooth Solomon's Seal can be found growing in the rich soil of woodlands, as well as along sunny roadsides—seeming to do equally well in both settings. It spreads by underground stems, or rhizomes, forming small colonies; but it does not become too aggressive or dominant.

COMMON NAME	**YELLOW CONEFLOWER**
BOTANICAL NAME	*Ratibida pinnata*
Height	2–4' (up to 5')
Spread	12"
Bloom time	Early summer to autumn
Flower	2", yellow head
Exposure	Full to partial sun
Soil moisture	Dry to wet
Spacing	8–12"

This plant, common to dry prairies and old fields, blooms from early summer to autumn. Its delicate foliage and flowers look good mixed with other wildflowers in the midborder or planted in sweeping masses with Indiangrass. No landscape should be without this plant's graceful, yellow blooms with drooping petals; thimble-sized seed heads add interest to the winter landscape and provide food for songbirds.

CULTURE Yellow Coneflower grows just about anywhere that receives a fair amount of sun, but it also does well in partly sunny locations. This fibrous-rooted plant tolerates dry to wet soils, sandy or clay, and can grow rather tall, up to 5 feet, if conditions are quite favorable. Drier sites produce shorter, more compact plants. In the absence of competition from other plants, Yellow Coneflower may grow too tall and flop over when in flower.

COMMON NAME	BLACK-EYED SUSAN
BOTANICAL NAME	*Rudbeckia hirta*
Height	12–24"
Spread	10"
Bloom time	Late spring to late summer
Flower	2", yellow head
Exposure	Full to partial sun
Soil moisture	Dry to mesic
Spacing	8–12"

Black-eyed Susan is a short-lived plant, but it is easy to grow from seed and produces a profusion of yellow flowers the first year. This plant can fill in the voids while other, longer-lived wildflowers take their time getting established in the landscape and are a year or more from flowering.
CULTURE In bloom from late spring until late summer, Black-eyed Susan should be seeded wherever immediate color is needed in the landscape. After the first year, plants freely self-sow and should be pulled out where necessary to keep the landscape looking its best. Plants may grow tall and weak-stemmed in rich soil but are carefree, forming compact plants on drier, poorer sites.

COMMON NAME	HAIRY WILD PETUNIA
BOTANICAL NAME	*Ruellia humilis*
Height	10"
Spread	Trailing
Bloom time	Early to late summer
Flower	1¹/₂", trumpet-shaped, pink
Exposure	Sun to partial shade
Soil moisture	Dry to mesic
Spacing	10"

Although not related to the annual petunia, Hairy Wild Petunia is similar in appearance, with its trailing habit, hairy leaves, and trumpet-shaped, pink flowers. But this petunia is a shade- and drought-tolerant plant that flowers for most of the growing season and requires very little care. It is good for covering those bare patches in the shade garden left by spring ephemerals such as the trilliums and White Trout Lily.
CULTURE This plant can be found growing in dry sites, in the full sun of a prairie, and in the partial shade of an upland woods. This petunia actually performs best with a little protection from full sun, so plant it in the shade garden or to the east or north of taller wildflowers. Hairy Wild Petunia appreciates a rich soil but also does well in sandy settings. Additional water in dry spells increases flowering, but plants suffer if soil is excessively moist, as may occur with irrigation.

COMMON NAME	**BLOODROOT**
BOTANICAL NAME	*Sanguinaria canadensis*
Height	8"
Spread	6"
Bloom time	Early spring
Flower	1", 8-petaled, white
Exposure	Partial to full shade
Soil moisture	Mesic
Spacing	10"

Bloodroot is an interesting and beautiful plant. Named for the orange–red latex within the leaves and roots, it emerges in early spring to produce pure white flowers. Soon after the flowers open, the water lily–like leaves, up to 8 inches across, unfurl—an interesting process to observe. As with most members of the poppy family, the flowers are short-lived, often shattering when touched, but the attractive foliage stays around as long as the soil is kept from drying out for an extended period.

CULTURE This tough plant is never overpowering despite its potentially large leaves. The numerous seeds produced are collected by ants and are spread throughout the garden. Bloodroot also forms colonies by underground, spreading stems, or rhizomes. To keep the foliage from yellowing in summer, mulch with 2 inches of shredded leaves to conserve soil moisture; however, the rhizomes may rot in excessively moist soil. This plant looks good planted throughout the garden, but do not plant it near the less competitive Sharp-lobed Hepatica, Jacob's Ladder, or the trilliums. Bloodroot is good interplanted with Virginia Bluebells. It blooms at the same time of year as Spring Beauty.

COMMON NAME	**PRAIRIE DOCK**
BOTANICAL NAME	*Silphium terebinthinaceum*
Height	24"
Spread	18–24"
Bloom time	Midsummer
Flower	2", yellow head
Exposure	Full sun
Soil moisture	Dry to wet
Spacing	12"

With its rosette of spade-shaped leaves—over a foot long and half again as wide—Prairie Dock never fails to make a bold statement in the landscape, while complementing other, finer-textured grasses and wildflowers. The plant itself reaches a height of only 2 feet, but in midsummer it sends up a 6- to 10-foot tall, single flower stalk topped by a cluster of 2-inch-wide yellow flowers—very dramatic yet not overpowering in a small garden. It is best used as a middle or foreground plant, grouped in clusters of three for greatest effect.

CULTURE Prairie Dock needs full sun but tolerates varying degrees of soil moisture and does well in heavy clay soils. This carefree plant spends its first few years developing an extensive root system before displaying its dramatic foliage.

COMMON NAME	**BLUE-EYED GRASS**
BOTANICAL NAME	*Sisyrinchium albidum*
Height	8–10"
Spread	8–12"
Bloom time	Late spring to early summer
Flower	¹/₂", star-shaped, blue or white
Exposure	Sun to partial shade
Soil moisture	Dry to mesic
Spacing	8"

Found in prairies and old pastures, Blue-eyed Grass is actually a member of the iris family and not a grass at all. Its half-inch, star-shaped flowers rising a few inches above the tuft of grasslike foliage open only on sunny mornings and close immediately upon being picked. It is an elegant little plant that charms those who slow down and take the time to look closely. It can be used as an edging plant or massed in small groups in the foreground. This plant is said to have been one of Thoreau's favorites.

CULTURE Although delicate in appearance, this plant is tough and thrives with benign neglect. Starting in late spring, it blooms for about a month and has attractive, ¹/₄-inch-wide, saberlike foliage all season. Its foliage develops best in the absence of competition, and it devotes most of its energy to foliage rather than flower production if the soil is too rich. If mulched, it may develop crown rot from too much moisture. Blue-eyed Grass appreciates the moisture of spring but otherwise does very well on dry sites in full sun. It is easily divided and replanted in early spring.

COMMON NAME	**STIFF GOLDENROD**
BOTANICAL NAME	*Oligoneuron rigidum*
Height	18"
Spread	18"
Bloom time	Late summer into fall
Flower	6", yellow cluster
Exposure	Sun
Soil moisture	Dry to mesic
Spacing	12"

Given the vast fields of what appears to be solid stands of goldenrod, it may seem unwise to introduce this species to the small landscape. Although many goldenrods spread aggressively by underground stems, Stiff Goldenrod is a rather well-behaved species, forming a rosette of gray–green leaves up to a foot long and 3 inches wide. In late summer, it sends up a 4-foot stalk topped by a 4- to 6-inch, flattopped cluster of small, yellow flowers. It is spectacular in the garden and a great cut flower.

CULTURE Place this plant in a dry or moist, sunny site; in sandy or clay soil; either singly or in groups of three. Allow room between plants so that the large leaves can spread out. It is best as a specimen plant, with shorter plants such as Prairie Alumroot, Blue-eyed Grass, or Penn Sedge around its base. This plant tends to be more aggressive and invasive in soils with consistent moisture. Remove the faded flowers to reduce spreading by seed although the dry seed heads are nice in winter arrangements. This goldenrod is one of the best for the small garden.

COMMON NAME	SPIDERWORT
BOTANICAL NAME	*Tradescantia virginiana*
Height	18–24"
Spread	12–18"
Bloom time	Midspring to early summer
Flower	¹/₂", 3-petaled, blue
Exposure	Sun to partial shade
Soil moisture	Dry to wet
Spacing	12"

The royal blue flowers of Spiderwort make for some spectacular color combinations with other wildflowers, such as Butterfly Milkweed, Pale Purple Coneflower, and Golden Alexanders. Each ¹/₂-inch flower lasts only a day, but buds are numerous in each cluster—enough to last a month or more. Spiderwort is a terrific accent plant.

CULTURE Spiderwort grows well in moist or dry sites; it even does well in shady locations. The plants are attractive for the first part of the growing season; but as midsummer approaches, they tend to yellow and may die back to the ground when grown in full sun. They are therefore best planted among other midheight plants to mask this effect.

COMMON NAME	WHITE TRILLIUM
BOTANICAL NAME	*Trillium grandiflorum*
Height	6–12"
Spread	4–8"
Bloom time	Midspring
Flower	2", 3-petaled, white
Exposure	Partial to full shade
Soil moisture	Mesic
Spacing	Random

Trilliums are beautiful spring ephemerals; and White Trillium, found in moist woods and floodplains, is one of the most striking. With its large, pure white flower sitting like a teacup on a saucer of three horizontally spread, green leaves teetering atop a one-foot-tall stem, White Trillium looks quite exotic and is a great addition to the shade garden.

CULTURE Trilliums prefer and do best in well-drained soil rich in organic matter, but they are not too fussy and flourish in most shady settings. Plants are shorter in drier locations; for taller plants, enrich the soil with compost and mulch with 2 inches of shredded leaves to conserve soil moisture. Trilliums slowly spread by long, horizontal rhizomes, forming small colonies; but they never look untidy or become a nuisance. Place this plant randomly throughout the garden, near a pathway where its flowers can best be appreciated. The plant goes dormant by midsummer, not to be seen again until the next spring. Mark the location of trilliums so as not to disturb them in dormancy.

COMMON NAME	**PRAIRIE TRILLIUM**
BOTANICAL NAME	*Trillium recurvatum*
Height	6–12"
Spread	4–8"
Bloom time	Midspring
Flower	1", 3-petaled, maroon
Exposure	Partial to full shade
Soil moisture	Mesic
Spacing	Random

Prairie Trillium is similar in habit to White Trillium but has a deep red flower and leaves mottled with shades of green and purple. It is an attractive plant that complements other springtime bloomers such as Trout Lily and Sharp-lobed Hepatica. This spring ephemeral forms small colonies from dispersed seed. The beauty of trilliums is best appreciated when space is left between them and other nearby plants.

CULTURE The culture is the same as for White Trillium.

NURSERY-GROWN VS. NURSERY-PROPAGATED

Trilliums and other woodland wildflowers are popular garden plants but are slow to mature into a salable product. Because of this trait, they are sometimes collected for sale from the wild, rather than being propagated in nurseries, and are thereby lost from our natural areas. Collected plants are often sold as "nursery-grown" after being tended in pots for a year. To protect against this highly unethical practice, ensure that every native plant you buy is "nursery-propagated," not merely nursery-grown.

COMMON NAME	**GOLDEN ALEXANDERS**
BOTANICAL NAME	*Zizia aurea*
Height	12–36"
Spread	12–18"
Bloom time	Mid- to late spring
Flower	4", chartreuse umbels
Exposure	Partial shade to sun
Soil moisture	Dry to mesic
Spacing	10"

This early flowering plant is up and blooming when many other wildflowers are just beginning to push up spring foliage. It is therefore best placed among Butterfly Milkweed, Yellow Coneflower, Purple Prairie Clover, and other later-blooming varieties. Its flattopped, chartreuse flowers look particularly good with the purple shades of Spiderwort and the early flowering Prairie Smoke. After blooming, the attractive, purple–bronze seed heads form and provide interest for the second half of the growing season. As a member of the carrot family, this plant provides food for swallowtail larvae.

CULTURE Found growing in sunny prairies as well as wooded stream floodplains, Golden Alexanders is a great early season bloomer for the sun or shade, moist or dry sites. It stays shorter and more compact in poor soils. This self-seeder sends up volunteers around the garden, but they are easily contained with a garden hoe early in the growing season.

GRASSES

COMMON NAME	**LITTLE BLUESTEM**
BOTANICAL NAME	*Schizachyrium scoparium [Andropogon scoparius]*
Height	18–48"
Spread	12–18"
Bloom time	Mid- to late summer
Flower	White tufts along 12" stalk
Exposure	Sun to partial shade
Soil moisture	Dry to mesic
Spacing	12"–24"

Found in sandy oak savannas, as well as dry and mesic prairies, this long-lived grass is a signature plant of the prairie. Little Bluestem is an upright-growing, short-statured bunchgrass with blue–green leaves. It is best planted in sweeping masses among wildflowers throughout the sunny landscape. Staying at about 18 inches for most of the summer, its height increases to 3 or 4 feet when in flower. The flowers in late summer, although not particularly showy, attract many butterflies; and the seeds are enjoyed by a variety of birds, including field sparrows and juncos. In autumn, the plant turns a nice reddish gold. This clump-forming grass does not spread aggressively and in small gardens is a good alternative to the much taller and less brilliant Big Bluestem. No prairie garden would be complete without Little Bluestem; it extends a landscape's season of interest from autumn into the winter months.

CULTURE Little Bluestem naturally occurs in well-drained sites with average soil moisture, in full sun or in the partial shade of an oak. It is not an aggressive spreader from its roots, which grow to depths of 5 or 6 feet; but you may see it coming up from seed in areas with open ground. The strong vertical habit and the blue–green leaves of this grass complement other wildflowers and grasses and should be used throughout the landscape as a unifying element.

BIG BLUESTEM, *Andropogon gerardii*
The tallgrass prairie gets its name, in part, because of Big Bluestem. This tall, 3- to 7-foot grass (its height depending on soil moisture) is a major constituent of the midwestern prairie. However, given its height, mass, and open habit, it is not well suited to the small landscape garden. For a touch of height and drama, Indiangrass is a more suitable and ornamental choice for the home landscape.

COMMON NAME	INDIANGRASS
BOTANICAL NAME	*Sorghastrum nutans [Chrysopogon nutans]*
Height	4–5'
Spread	24"
Bloom time	Late summer
Flower	6", golden panicle
Exposure	Sun to partial shade
Soil moisture	Dry to mesic
Spacing	18"

Indiangrass is one of the most ornamental and majestic tall prairie grasses and is excellent in the small home landscape. It forms a more upright plant than Big Bluestem, with lighter, blue–green foliage that stands out from and complements the darker greens of other plants. In late summer, this grass produces showy, 6- to 10-inch, copper-colored plumes atop 4- to 5-foot stems. In autumn, the foliage turns a nice golden color. The foliage and seed heads are attractive throughout the winter months. Several species of butterflies use Indiangrass as a source of food, and many birds enjoy the seeds. This grass is best planted in groups of three or five and bordered by Prairie Dropseed or midheight wildflowers such as Yellow Coneflower, Rattlesnake Master, Pale Purple Coneflower, and Aromatic Aster.
CULTURE This carefree grass is found in both mesic and dry prairies and in open woods. It tolerates clay but prefers a well-drained soil and is quite drought-tolerant once its roots, which go to depths of 6 feet, are established. This beautiful plant with good winter presence is a real asset to any landscape.

COMMON NAME	PRAIRIE DROPSEED
BOTANICAL NAME	*Sporobolus heterolepis*
Height	12"
Spread	24"
Bloom time	Late summer
Flower	8" raceme of spikelets
Exposure	Sun to partial shade
Soil moisture	Dry to mesic
Spacing	18–24"

An effective and ornamental grass in the home landscape, Prairie Dropseed's fountain of very narrow leaves catches the slightest summer breeze, giving an illusion of undulating water. In autumn, the leaves turn pinkish gold, ultimately becoming an attractive straw brown in winter. A profusion of flowers appears at the end of summer, very showy and smelling of cilantro. This plant works best when massed in the foreground in groups of five or more. It provides a good transition from prairie plants to turfgrass.
CULTURE Naturally occurring in many prairie types, as well as in sandy savannas, this undemanding grass does well in full sun or partial shade as long as the soil is well-drained. Prairie Dropseed is slow to show mature top growth until its extensive root system, reaching to depths of 5 feet or more, is established. Interplant with Hairy Wild Petunia to fill voids while waiting for them to reach full size rather than crowding plants by reducing spacing.

SEDGES

More than 100 species of sedges occur naturally in the Midwest, but these attractive, grasslike plants are often overlooked when it comes to designing the home landscape. This tendency is unfortunate because sedges are great plants that can add interest and dynamic appeal to any landscape and attract a wide range of songbirds, including cardinals, finches, juncos, and sparrows. The first step in appreciating sedges is knowing what they look like: This task is not always easy, given their diversity, but it can be done.

Many sedges flower in mid- to late spring; this is the best time to separate the grasses from the sedges. To identify a plant as a sedge, look for grasslike leaves that emerge in groups of three from a flowering stem; the leaves of grass emerge in pairs. Likewise, grasses have round, hollow, flowering stems; sedges have triangular, solid, flowering stems; as the saying goes, "sedges have edges." Once you are able to identify sedges, you appreciate their diversity of form, adaptability to various growing situations, and overall beauty out in the wild. You also come to realize their potential in the home landscape. The following three sedges are just a few of the many that look great and do well in the home landscape.

COMMON NAME	PENN SEDGE
BOTANICAL NAME	*Carex pensylvanica*
Height	6–8"
Spread	8"
Bloom time	Early spring
Flower	$1/2$", brown spike
Exposure	Partial shade to sun
Soil moisture	Dry to mesic
Spacing	6–8"

Although most sedges prefer consistently moist soils, Penn Sedge commonly occurs in both dry woods and prairies. This plant greens up early in spring, giving the appearance of a bright green lawn before other plants emerge and become dominant. Useful in many situations, Penn Sedge, as well as other sedges such as Grass Sedge, should be encouraged to grow throughout both woodland and prairie settings. Woodland plants, such as Jack-in-the-Pulpit, Woodland Phlox, and Smooth Solomon's Seal, look great growing up through Penn Sedge's short, grasslike leaves. The narrow leaves, $1/16$ to $1/8$ inch wide, turn a nice sandy tan in the fall.

CULTURE Plant Penn Sedge in full sun or partial shade. It tolerates most soil types from clay to sandy. It forms a good, 6- to 8-inch-tall groundcover if competition from other, more aggressive plants is reduced. No landscape should be without a few sedge species; they add the finishing touch otherwise missing in many designed landscapes.

PRAIRIE SEDGE, *Carex bicknellii*
Found in dry prairies and open woods, Prairie Sedge grows in association with most of the upland wildflowers and grasses, including Leadplant, Rattlesnake Master, Flowering Spurge, Rough Blazing Star, Little Bluestem, and Indiangrass. When placed 12 inches apart in moist or dry soil, the

plants form a shimmering 18-inch-tall fountain of $^1/_8$-inch leaves, with clusters of $^1/_2$-inch spikelets appearing atop 3-foot stems in mid- to late spring. This sedge is very effective when planted in sweeping masses or among midheight wildflowers such as Yellow Coneflower.

GRASS SEDGE, *Carex jamesii*
Grass Sedge forms a fountain of $^1/_8$-inch-wide leaves 6 inches tall. This sedge can be found growing in woodlands under Sugar Maples and oaks and in yards, where grass has failed to thrive in the shade of mature trees. Single plants form attractive clumps with small, spiky seed heads rising just above the foliage in midspring. If encouraged, this sedge forms an almost solid, turflike mass under shade trees. Grass Sedge tolerates a fair amount of sun but prefers shade. Dry soils are not a problem for this sedge.

FERNS

COMMON NAME	MAIDENHAIR FERN
BOTANICAL NAME	*Adiantum pedatum*
Height	12"
Spread	12"
Exposure	Partial to full shade
Soil moisture	Mesic
Spacing	12"

Maidenhair Fern can be found growing in moist, rich, well-drained woods and streamsides; but this adaptable and carefree fern also does quite well in the drier conditions found in many yards. The finely divided, fan-shaped leaves spread horizontally atop a one-foot-tall black stem and flutter in the slightest breeze, seeming to float just above the surface of the soil. Its delicate and airy appearance belies the fact that this fern is tough and easy to grow.

CULTURE This fern prefers to grow in partial to deep shade but can tolerate quite a bit of sun if the soil is kept moist; in shady sites, it is more tolerant of dry soils. In any case, it may go dormant in periods of extended drought. Therefore, it is a good idea to keep Maidenhair Fern mulched with 2 inches of shredded leaves to conserve soil moisture. It forms loose colonies and complements coarser-leafed plants such as Woodland Ginger and Sharp-lobed Hepatica. Underplant with White Trout Lily or Spring Beauty.

COMMON NAME	**CHRISTMAS FERN**
BOTANICAL NAME	*Polystichum acrostichoides*
Height	12"
Spread	18"
Exposure	Partial to full shade
Soil moisture	Dry to mesic
Spacing	18"

Christmas Fern, named for its use by pioneers as a holiday decoration, is one of the most attractive and forgiving ferns for the shade garden. The foot-long, arching fronds of leathery foliage are so perfect and glossy green all season, even into winter, that some people may wonder if the plants are artificial. This fern is one of the few that do not turn yellow when soils dry out in midsummer. Planted randomly in masses of three or five, Christmas Fern can make even a poorly thought-out shade garden look good.

CULTURE Growing in wooded dunes as well as rich mesic woods, this fern does well in just about any shady location. It appreciates additional organic matter dug into the soil and a 2-inch layer of shredded leaf mulch; but once established, it is quite drought-tolerant. It slowly spreads by creeping underground stems, but control does not become a problem.

SHRUBS

COMMON NAME	**LEADPLANT**
BOTANICAL NAME	*Amorpha canescens*
Height	12–18"
Spread	30"
Bloom time	Midsummer
Flower	4", violet raceme
Exposure	Sun to partial shade
Soil moisture	Dry to mesic
Spacing	24"

This attractive, low-growing, prairie shrub has finely divided, hairy, silvery gray leaves. In midsummer, branch tips are covered with elongated clusters of small, violet flowers with prominent, orange anthers. The silvery foliage contrasts with and complements the leaves of adjacent wildflowers and grasses. As a legume, it enriches the soil with nitrogen it takes from the air. It looks good in front of Indiangrass and between swaths of wildflowers.

CULTURE Found in dry and mesic prairies, as well as sandy savannas, Leadplant likes well-drained soil, in full sun or light shade. The deep taproot makes the shrub drought-tolerant and carefree once established but also difficult to move as a mature plant.

COMMON NAME	BLACK CHOKEBERRY
BOTANICAL NAME	Aronia melanocarpa [A. prunifolia]
Height	3–6'
Spread	3–6'
Bloom time	Midspring
Flower	2", white cluster
Exposure	Sun to partial shade
Soil moisture	Wet to dry
Fall color	Red

Black Chokeberry is an attractive shrub that grows under a wide range of conditions. It works well as a shrub growing to about 6 feet or a sheared hedge. In spring, it is covered by clusters of small, white flowers, followed by black berries that are enjoyed by many birds, including cedar waxwings and meadowlarks, as well as other wildlife. In autumn, the leaves turn crimson; this effect is especially pronounced when Black Chokeberry is grown in full sun.

CULTURE Black Chokeberry grows in poorly drained clay to well-drained, sandy soil, in full sun to partial shade. In addition, it is tolerant of flooded ground, compacted soil, and road salt. It prefers moist soil with a slightly acidic pH, 5.1 to 6.5. Its fibrous root system allows it to be transplanted easily. In drier sites, lay down 3 inches of mulch to conserve soil moisture and reduce transplant stress, allowing it to become established more quickly.

COMMON NAME	NEW JERSEY TEA
BOTANICAL NAME	Ceanothus americanus
Height	1–3'
Spread	3–6'
Bloom time	Late spring to early summer
Flower	2", white spike
Exposure	Sun to partial shade
Soil moisture	Dry to mesic
Fall color	Yellow/brown

New Jersey Tea is a terrific, low-growing shrub for either sun or partial shade. Forming colonies, it produces a dense mass of upright stems with leathery, dark green, one-inch-long, ovate leaves. Although lacking good fall color, it is covered by oblong clusters of small, white flowers in early summer, followed by small, brown seed capsules. Hummingbirds are attracted to the flowers, getting their protein from the pollinating insects found there. Used in front of taller wildflowers and grasses, it provides a good transition from prairie plantings to lawn.

CULTURE Demonstrating its adaptability, New Jersey Tea is widely distributed and can be found growing in shady Black Oak savannas, sand dunes, and mesic and dry prairies. Its adaptability is due, in part, to its massive, woody root system and its ability to fix nitrogen from the air. Although it prefers an acidic, well-drained soil with a pH of 4.5 to 6.0, it is tolerant of a wide range of soils, from sandy to clay. It has some tolerance of road salt and is drought-tolerant once established. It is, however, a favorite food of rabbits and deer and when young may need to be protected. The only pruning needed may be to remove a few branches that have died back over the winter. It has no serious insect or disease problems.

COMMON NAME	**GRAY DOGWOOD**
BOTANICAL NAME	*Cornus racemosa*
Height	6–10'
Spread	8–12'
Bloom time	Late spring
Flower	2", white clusters
Exposure	Full to partial sun
Soil moisture	Dry to wet
Fall color	Purple/red

Found in prairies and woodland edges, Gray Dogwood forms a colony of strongly vertical gray stems from a spreading root system. These colonies of about 50 square feet, have stems 1/2-inch across, spaced a foot or so apart, and finely branched near the top. The result looks like a miniature tree grove and provides an attractive background for prairie wildflowers and grasses. It also looks great underplanted with shade-tolerant plants such as Woodland Geranium, Mayapple, Hairy Wild Petunia, Scarlet Strawberry, Penn Sedge, or Grass Sedge. The 2-inch, narrow, elliptic leaves are a nice gray–green with a silvery underside, creating an effective play of light when fluttering in a breeze. In late spring, the plants are covered with creamy white flower clusters, followed by small, white fruit that is readily eaten by birds, including cardinals, crows, cedar waxwings, and bluebirds. In autumn, the leaves turn a nice reddish purple; and the finely branched, upright stems look especially attractive in winter. Gray Dogwood is best used where its spreading tendencies will not become a problem or where its spread is constrained by pavement, the shade of nearby trees, or a maintained lawn.

CULTURE Gray Dogwood grows in a wide range of soil types (from well-drained, sandy soils to poorly drained, clay soil) in full or part sun. It prefers moist, sunny sites but stays shorter and spreads less in drier locations. As new shoots appear, prune them to the ground to contain a colony's spread to a smaller area. A colony of Gray Dogwood surrounded by a 4-foot-wide mixed border of 70 percent Little Bluestem interplanted with a 30 percent mix of prairie wildflowers—such as Purple Prairie Clover, Foxglove Beard Tongue, Flowering Spurge, and Yellow Coneflower—looks great from spring through to winter.

COMMON NAME	RED OSIER DOGWOOD
BOTANICAL NAME	*Cornus stolonifera [C. sericea]*
Height	4–10'
Spread	4–10'
Bloom time	Late spring
Flower	2", cream cluster
Exposure	Sun
Soil moisture	Wet to dry
Fall color	Orange/red/purple

Red Osier Dogwood is noticed by most people during winter, when its bright red stems stand out against a fresh blanket of snow; but it is also nice during the growing season. In spring, and sporadically throughout the summer, its branches are topped by creamy white flower clusters, followed by small, white fruit that are enjoyed by shorebirds and waterfowl. In autumn, the 2-inch, oval leaves turn a nice orange–red. It is very attractive with Prairie Dropseed and Waukegan Creeping Juniper planted at its base.

CULTURE Red Osier Dogwood does well in most sunny sites but is quite intolerant of shade. Found growing along the sand dunes of Lake Michigan, this plant prefers moist, well-drained sites but is adaptable to a wide range of growing conditions, including poor to well-drained soils and those slightly acidic (pH 6.1) to alkaline (pH 8.5). It is also tolerant of drought, flooding, and compacted soil but sensitive to road salt. Once the plant is established, one-third of the older stems should be cut back to the ground every November. This practice keeps the plant from becoming overgrown, encourages flowering on young growth, ensures a good supply of new red stems every winter, and reduces problems from stem cankers and borers.

COMMON NAME	KALM'S ST. JOHNS-WORT
BOTANICAL NAME	*Hypericum kalmianum*
Height	2–3'
Spread	2–3'
Bloom time	Late spring
Flower	1", yellow
Exposure	Sun
Soil moisture	Wet to dry
Fall color	Yellow/green

Kalm's St. Johns-wort is an attractive, small-mounded shrub with spectacular, bright yellow flowers in late spring to early summer. It is fine-textured, with linear leaves less than 2 inches by ¼ inch. St. Johns-wort looks good planted with Black Chokeberry behind and Waukegan Creeping Juniper in front. The word *wort* is derived from Old English, meaning plant.

CULTURE Naturally found growing along the edge of interdunal ponds near Lake Michigan, as well as on cliffs above streams and lakes, St. Johns-wort is adaptable to a wide range of soil conditions but needs full sun to do well. It grows in well-drained, sandy soil or poorly drained, clay soil. It is resistant to drought and road salt and toleratess soil compaction, flooding, and soils with a pH of 5.1 to 8.5. Its fibrous root system allows it to be transplanted easily. Although the plant itself is naturally short-lived, it has no serious insect or disease problems, and is a good choice for the sunny landscape.

COMMON NAME	**WINTERBERRY HOLLY**
BOTANICAL NAME	*Ilex verticillata*
Height	5–8'
Spread	4–6'
Bloom time	Late spring
Flower	¹/₄", greenish white
Exposure	Partial shade to sun
Soil moisture	Mesic to wet
Fall color	Yellow/brown

Winterberry Holly gets its common name from its unsurpassed display of small, red berries in autumn, which last to the holiday season. By the start of the new year, songbirds (especially thrushes, mockingbird, robin, bluebird, and thrasher) eat the fruit, or freezing temperatures cause them to drop. But even after the fruit has gone, the gnarly, oaklike branches have an interesting character.

CULTURE Found growing in flatwoods and bogs along with Black Choke-berry, Black Tupelo, and White Pine, Winterberry Holly is easy to transplant but a bit particular about where it grows. It does not like hot, dry, sunny locations; it does best in sites with partial shade and moist, preferably acidic, soil. If the soil pH is too alkaline, higher than 8.0, the plant suffers and the leaves yellow. It is tolerant of most soil types from sandy to clay, of soil compaction, and of flooding; it does well in full sun if the soil has at least average moisture and it is not planted near heat-reflecting pavement. To get a display of fruit, fruiting female plants and at least one pollinating male plant are needed. It has no serious insect or disease problems.

COMMON NAME	**WAUKEGAN CREEPING JUNIPER**
BOTANICAL NAME	*Juniperus horizontalis* var. *douglasii*
Height	6–12"
Spread	5–10'
Bloom time	Early spring
Flower	Small, not showy
Exposure	Sun
Soil moisture	Dry to mesic
Fall color	Evergreen

Found growing along Lake Michigan shores with Little Bluestem, Flowering Spurge, Purple Prairie Clover, and Pasture Rose, this low-growing juniper also creates a nice evergreen groundcover for the sunny home landscape. The blue–green plumes of foliage turn shades of purple in winter; and its small, gray, berrylike cones are eaten by songbirds, including the cedar wax-wing, purple finch, and bluebird, and by other wildlife. This good foreground plant creates a pleasing transition from prairie plantings to lawn.

CULTURE Waukegan Creeping Juniper thrives in hot, dry, sunny locations and is quite intolerant of shade and poorly drained soil. It does well in soils with a pH of 5.0 to 8.5, moderate to excessive drainage, and average to droughty moisture levels. Several disease and insect problems affect junipers, including bagworm and cedar–apple rust, but they do not commonly create a problem in the home landscape.

COMMON NAME	DWARF FRAGRANT SUMAC
BOTANICAL NAME	*Rhus aromatica* var. *arenaria*
Height	2–4'
Spread	4–6'
Bloom time	Midspring
Flower	1" catkins
Exposure	Sun to partial sun
Soil moisture	Dry to mesic
Fall color	Orange/red/purple

Dwarf Fragrant Sumac is an attractive, low-growing shrub for the sunny landscape. The three-parted, aromatic leaves are a subtle blue–green, turning shades of orange, red, and purple in autumn. Female plants have small clusters of fuzzy, red fruit rich in provitamin A that are an important source of winter food for birds and other wildlife. This plant is good in the foreground wherever it receives plenty of sun. It makes a nice transition from lawn to prairie plantings.

CULTURE Commonly found in dunes and Black Oak savannas, as well as open prairies, Dwarf Fragrant Sumac prefers an open, sunny to partly sunny, well-drained location with average to droughty soil moisture. Soil pH can range from 6.1 to 8.5, but plants prefer a slightly acidic soil. It does not do well in compacted soil, shade, or flood-prone areas. The fibrous root system makes this plant easy to transplant successfully, and its trailing stems self-root. Dwarf Fragrant Sumac has no serious insect or disease problems.

COMMON NAME	PASTURE ROSE
BOTANICAL NAME	*Rosa carolina*
Height	1–2'
Spread	4–8'
Bloom time	Late spring to midsummmer
Flower	2", deep pink
Exposure	Sun to partial sun
Soil moisture	Dry to wet
Fall color	Yellow/orange/red

Commonly found in dry, open prairies and woodland edges, Pasture Rose is a terrific, low-growing rose for the sunny border. It forms mounds of dense foliage with fragrant, pink flowers appearing in the first half of the growing season, followed by small, red fruit (rich in vitamin C) that are eaten by birds and other wildlife. Place Pasture Rose along the edge of other plantings, such as prairie wildflowers and grasses, Blackhaw Viburnum, Downy Serviceberry, or Black Chokeberry, for a pleasing effect.

CULTURE Pasture Rose grows in sun to partial sun, in sandy, loam, or clay soil. It thrives in heat and drought and does not mind some soil compaction but is sensitive to road salt. It tolerates soils with a pH of 6.1 to 8.5. The shallow, fibrous roots can form colonies by sending up shoots as they spread. This spreading can be kept in check if necessary by pruning back shoots as they appear. Plants tend to spread more in moist or irrigated sites, where stems are more likely to root as they touch the ground. Pasture Rose is occasionally affected by insects and diseases such as rusts, black spot, and aphids but is generally a carefree, attractive plant.

COMMON NAME	ELDERBERRY
BOTANICAL NAME	*Sambucus canadensis*
Height	5–12'
Spread	6–12'
Bloom time	Early summer
Flower	6–8", white cluster
Exposure	Sun to shade
Soil moisture	Mesic
Fall color	Yellow/green

Not a diminutive plant, Elderberry makes a bold statement in the home landscape. The leaves are a foot long and made up of half a dozen or so leaflets, each about 2 inches long and an inch wide. The flowers appear in early summer and form white clusters as broad as an outspread hand, followed in late summer by blue–black berries that are an important summer food source for many birds, including the redheaded and red-bellied wood-peckers. Although Elderberry is a very attractive plant, it needs room to develop to its full potential.

CULTURE Elderberry can be found growing just about anywhere, in full sun and well-drained soil or in low, wet areas in shade. It is most attractive when grown in full sun, where it forms a dense shrub and more flowers. Impatiently leafing out in early spring, it is also a fast grower, putting on 3 feet or more in one season, and can become overpowering if grown in a tight space. Older stems may require cutting back to the ground to keep the plant about 6 feet in height. An attractive specimen planted in full sun, Elderberry produces a more open habit in shade. It is very nice when grown along a woodland edge in association with woodland wildflowers.

TREES

COMMON NAME	SUGAR MAPLE
BOTANICAL NAME	*Acer saccharum*
Height	60–70'
Spread	50–75'
Habit	Oval to rounded
Exposure	Sun to partial shade
Soil moisture	Mesic
Fall color	Yellow/orange/red

Sugar Maple is a long-lived, large shade tree that forms a symmetrically rounded, dense crown of foliage that displays an unequaled blaze of color in autumn. It produces a nice shade tree but needs room for its extensive roots and crown of branches to spread. Its roots, however, do not generally lift sidewalks or clog drainpipes; and except for very hot, dry sites, it is an excellent choice for the home landscape.

CULTURE Unlike its floodplain relatives [the Red Maple *(Acer rubrum)* and the Silver Maple *(Acer saccharinum)*], Sugar Maple is an upland forest tree of mesic woods and consequently prefers a soil with good to average soil moisture but not soil that is compacted, excessively moist, or flood prone. Sugar Maples are apt to show signs of transplant stress and leaf scald if planted in full sun without adequate soil moisture. Partially shaded sites are preferred by young Sugar Maples in the wild, but full-sun sites are not a problem if soil moisture is consistent and the tree does not receive reflected heat from masonry buildings or pavement. A 3-foot-wide ring of 3-inch-deep mulch around the base of a young tree helps conserve soil moisture and eliminate root competition from turfgrass. Sugar Maple is pH adaptable, has a moderate growth rate, and is rarely bothered by insect or disease problems. Avoid locations where exposure to road salt causes moisture stress.

COMMON NAME	**DOWNY SERVICEBERRY**
BOTANICAL NAME	*Amelanchier arborea*
Height	15–25'
Spread	10–20'
Bloom time	Early spring
Flower	3", white raceme
Exposure	Shade to sun
Soil moisture	Dry to mesic
Fall color	Red/orange/yellow

Downy Serviceberry can be grown as a small tree with one, two, or three trunks or as a many-stemmed shrub; it grows taller as a single-stemmed tree. Either way, it forms a nice, airy canopy of blue–green leaves above stems with attractive, smooth, gray bark. In early spring, before the leaves emerge, it is covered by clusters of small, white flowers—blooming just before Eastern Redbud. In June, the dark blue fruit similar to blueberries in taste and appearance ripen and are readily eaten by songbirds. In autumn, the leaves turn shades of red, orange, and yellow. In winter its elegant branching pattern stands out. Grown as a shrub or small tree, Downy Serviceberry makes a very nice specimen underplanted with wildflowers.

CULTURE Found growing along stream banks, dry upland woods, and high dunes, Downy Serviceberry is quite adaptable and thrives in a wide range of conditions. It prefers well-drained soil that is slightly acidic but does equally well in dense shade or full sun. This plant has a moderate growth rate of 12 to 18 inches a year when young and is easy to transplant. It has a good branching structure, never looks messy, and rarely needs pruning. It is a carefree plant that looks good year-round.

COMMON NAME	**RIVER BIRCH**
BOTANICAL NAME	*Betula nigra*
Height	40–70'
Spread	40–60'
Habit	Rounded–pyramidal in youth; rounded with age
Exposure	Sun
Soil moisture	Mesic to wet
Fall color	Yellow

River Birch can be found growing in open, sunny places along slow-moving streams and at the edge of wetlands in sand prairies. Best when grown with multiple trunks of three or four, it forms a beautiful ornamental tree with creamy white, tan, and brown exfoliating bark and pendulous branches with leaves that flutter in the lightest breeze. Planted as a single specimen or repeated through the landscape, it forms a beautiful backdrop to other prairie plantings.

CULTURE South of Wisconsin, Paper Birch and Gray Birch *(Betula papyrifera* and *B. populifolia)* suffer insect and disease problems related to heat stress, but the equally ornamental River Birch is adapted to deal with heat and periods of drought, as well as flooding and compacted soil, with no complaints. It prefers soil with adequate moisture and a slightly acidic to neutral pH. Its fibrous root system allows it to be transplanted easily in spring or late autumn. It has no major insect or disease problems and is resistant to bronze birch borer—an insect that frequently attacks and kills Paper Birch and Gray Birch.

COMMON NAME	BLUE BEECH
BOTANICAL NAME	*Carpinus caroliniana*
Height	20–30'
Spread	20–30'
Habit	Rounded
Exposure	Partial shade
Soil moisture	Mesic to wet
Fall color	Yellow/orange/red

Blue Beech is named for its attractive, smooth, gray bark resembling that of a beech tree. This low-branched, shrubby tree is often seen growing along the edge of streams in the shade of Red Oak, White Oak, and Sugar Maple. Its autumn foliage is variable but ranges from yellow–orange to red. In midspring, its catkins open and elongate, looking like little caterpillars hanging from the tips of the branches. The insignificant female flowers later transform into ornamental, light green, three-winged nutlets. Its low, dense crown of foliage can be used to screen unwanted views, as well as provide a place to nestle a woodland wildflower garden soon after the tree has been planted.

CULTURE This slow-growing tree prefers moist soil and partial shade but does well in a sunny site with an eastern exposure and average soil moisture. Blue Beech is difficult to transplant in larger sizes, with the smaller plants best transplanted in the spring. It is carefree and generally not affected by insects or disease. The lower limbs can be removed to reveal its attractive bark and to allow more light to reach the shade plants below.

COMMON NAME	**EASTERN REDBUD**
BOTANICAL NAME	*Cercis canadensis*
Height	20–30'
Spread	25–35'
Bloom time	Early spring
Flower	1", rosy pink
Exposure	Sun to partial shade
Soil moisture	Average to mesic
Fall color	Yellow/green

Eastern Redbud is a small, ornamental tree often found growing along moist woodland edges, especially in the more southerly portions of the tallgrass prairie region, but it naturally occurs as far north as southern Michigan and Chicago. It forms a picturesque crown of gnarly branches with 3-inch-wide, heart-shaped leaves; but even before the leaves appear, the branches are covered with clusters of deep pink, pea-like flowers in early spring at the same time as Serviceberry blooms. Redbud is a great accent plant and grows to fit its space. A nice display is produced when Redbud is underplanted with early spring–flowering wildflowers such as Virginia Bluebells, Bloodroot, Spring Beauty, and White Trout Lily.

CULTURE Redbud is adaptable to a range of growing conditions and does well in most soils. It is indifferent to soil pH but prefers moist, not wet, well-drained soil and can be grown in full sun or partial shade. With increased sunlight exposure, it forms a more dense crown and a greater number of blooms. Redbud can be short-lived, however, and is susceptible to several diseases, including verticillium wilt and canker. Still, it is a tree worthy of planting (and replanting every 15 years or so). And even though Redbud can be cold hardy into Minnesota, this property varies according to the origin of a particular tree or cultivar. Trees from Tennessee, or even southern Illinois, for example, may not be cold hardy in the Chicago area. Redbud, however, is easily transplanted and moderately fast-growing at a foot or more a year; volunteer seedlings from a nearby friend's tree can be a good source of cold-hardy plant material for your yard. Seedlings are best transplanted in autumn, after their first year of growth. Nursery-grown trees can be planted in the spring or autumn.

COMMON NAME	**PAGODA DOGWOOD**
BOTANICAL NAME	*Cornus alternifolia*
Height	15–25'
Spread	15–25'
Bloom time	Midspring
Flower	2", cream cluster
Exposure	Full to partial shade
Soil moisture	Mesic
Fall color	Purple

Growing one-and-a-half times wider than its height, Pagoda Dogwood can be considered a low-branched, small tree or a large shrub. The horizontally layered limbs are covered with fragrant, creamy white clusters of flowers, followed by ¼-inch, black fruit. In autumn, the leaves turn a deep purple–

red, contrasting nicely with the red leaves of Black Chokeberry and the yellow leaves of Downy Serviceberry. Pagoda Dogwood makes a nice, low-growing tree for a shady part of the landscape.

CULTURE As an understory tree, Pagoda Dogwood prefers a moist, shady location and suffers if it receives too much direct sun or is exposed to reflected heat from nearby masonry walls or pavement. It performs best in a site with an eastern or northern exposure. It becomes established more quickly and with less difficulty if transplanted as a young plant and where its roots are kept cool. Once established, it has a moderate growth rate and rarely needs pruning. Pagoda Dogwood is a truly beautiful plant if kept out of sunny, dry locations.

COMMON NAME	THORNLESS COCKSPUR HAWTHORN
BOTANICAL NAME	*Crataegus crusgalli* var. *inermis*
Height	8–12'
Spread	15–25'
Bloom time	Midspring
Flower	2", white cluster
Exposure	Sun to partial shade
Soil moisture	Dry to mesic
Fall color	Orange/red

Cockspur Hawthorn can be found growing along the edge of prairies, where grassland meets woodland. The species forms a small, flattopped tree with a dense crown of thorny branches. The 3-inch-long thorns, while protecting nesting birds from predators such as house cats and raccoons, can also injure people; therefore, in most home landscapes, the thornless variety is recommended. In summer, its 1- to 2-inch-long, dark green, glossy leaves create an effective background for prairie wildflowers and grasses; in autumn, the leaves turn a nice orange–red. As the leaves fall, its small, crabapple-like, red fruit is displayed on the tightly knit, horizontally layered branches, creating a nice display throughout winter. In spring, the branches are covered with 2-inch, flattopped clusters of small, white flowers. This tree looks good with a single trunk or multiple stems, but place it far enough away from structures so that its spreading crown is not impeded.

CULTURE Cockspur Hawthorn, including the thornless variety, is not too particular about where it grows. Any well-drained site in full sun or partial shade is fine. It is pH adaptable and tolerant of drought and occasional flooding. Urban pollution does not phase it. Several insect and disease problems affect most hawthorns, but they are usually not severe or common enough to detract from the overall beauty of this tree. Cockspur Hawthorns are best transplanted in early spring.

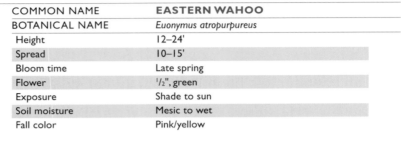

COMMON NAME	**EASTERN WAHOO**
BOTANICAL NAME	*Euonymus atropurpureus*
Height	12–24'
Spread	10–15'
Bloom time	Late spring
Flower	¹/₂", green
Exposure	Shade to sun
Soil moisture	Mesic to wet
Fall color	Pink/yellow

As a relative of the Asian Dwarf Burning Bush *(Euonymus alatus* 'Compactus'), which is often seen in home landscapes, Eastern Wahoo has many of the same adaptable qualities. However, it attains a more graceful form in maturity and puts on an eye-catching autumn show of pink and yellow foliage. In addition, it has persistent, small, neon pink seed capsules that give the appearance of pink flowers in October, the seeds of which are enjoyed by songbirds, including cardinals and robins. This plant can be grown as a single-stemmed, 12-foot-tall tree with slightly weeping branches or a 6-foot-tall, multi-stemmed shrub; or it can even be pruned into a dense hedge. In whatever form grown, Eastern Wahoo is an attractive and interesting addition to the home landscape.

CULTURE As mentioned, Eastern Wahoo is adaptable to a wide range of growing conditions, from clay to rich loam and in full sun or partial shade. Poorly drained soil is no problem, and it is somewhat tolerant of soil compaction and drought. It prefers to grow in partial shade, in moist soil with a neutral pH between 6.6 and 7.5. The dense, fibrous root system makes it easy to transplant successfully; and once established, it has a growth rate of about 18 inches a year. It has few insect or disease problems—other than scale, which requires treatment if found.

COMMON NAME	**BLUE ASH**
BOTANICAL NAME	*Fraxinus quadrangulata*
Height	50–70'
Spread	30–50'
Habit	Oval to rounded
Exposure	Sun
Soil moisture	Dry to mesic
Fall color	Yellow

Blue Ash, unlike its lowland relatives the Green Ash *(Fraxinus pennsylvanica)* and White Ash *(F. americana),* is more commonly found in dry, calcareous, upland sites. Although the other two ashes do fine in average soil, Blue Ash thrives in dry, alkaline soils. It produces a medium-sized shade tree that is also quite ornamental, with finely divided platy bark and an attractive, almost tropical-looking crown of foliage on square, winged stems. It has a consistently straight, central leader, something that cannot be said for the often-leaning Green Ash; and its pinnately divided leaves have distinctly narrow and attractive leaflets, more narrow than either those of Green Ash or White Ash. Blue Ash gets its name from its inner bark, which turns blue upon exposure to the air.

CULTURE At a rate of about one foot a year, Blue Ash grows more slowly than the other two ashes mentioned; but it is more drought-tolerant than either Green Ash or White Ash. Also unique is its ability to thrive in alkaline soils, a condition often found on new house sites where clay is abundant. Ashes are susceptible to a number of insects and diseases, but many infestations are probably due to stressed, lowland trees being planted in dry, upland sites. Blue Ash can live to 150 years and is a generally carefree tree.

COMMON NAME	**KENTUCKY COFFEETREE**
BOTANICAL NAME	*Gymnocladus dioica [G. dioicus]*
Height	60–75'
Spread	40–50'
Habit	Oval to rounded
Exposure	Sun
Soil moisture	Mesic
Fall color	Yellow

Kentucky Coffeetree is widely scattered throughout the tallgrass prairie region. It is believed that many specimens found by early pioneers were purposefully or inadvertently planted by American Indians who carried and traded the tree's large, flat, round seeds for game pieces or other purposes. The pioneers learned to use the seeds as a coffee substitute, hence its common name. The bipinnately divided leaves, which appear in late May, give the tree a fine, or soft, texture in summer and disguise a coarse but interesting branching pattern that is revealed in winter. The trunk has scalelike bark with cupped edges, creating an interesting if not ornamental feature. There are separate male and female trees. In June, the female trees have beautifully rose-scented flowers that later produce 6-inch-long by 2-inch-wide seed pods, which add interest, as they tend to persist on the tree through winter. The pods are not so numerous as to create a major litter problem as they fall to the ground. Kentucky Coffeetree is an effective shade tree that is also highly ornamental.

CULTURE Kentucky Coffeetree can be found growing in calcareous woods, along with Blue Ash and Eastern Redbud. It likes a site that receives full sun and has adequate soil moisture. It is an adaptable tree, tolerant of droughty conditions, soils with a neutral to alkaline pH, urban air pollution, and road salt. It is usually not bothered by insect or disease problems and takes hot or cold weather in stride. It can be difficult to transplant and may be 6 feet tall before sending out side branches, giving it an awkward appearance in youth. Kentucky Coffeetree grows about 12 feet in 10 years.

COMMON NAME	**WITCH-HAZEL**
BOTANICAL NAME	*Hamamelis virginiana*
Height	15–20'
Spread	15–25'
Bloom time	Midautumn
Flower	1", yellow
Exposure	Shade to partial shade
Soil moisture	Mesic
Fall color	Yellow

Witch-hazel is a small tree or large shrub that forms a picturesquely branched, broad crown with oval to rounded, 4-inch leaves that turn a golden yellow in autumn. Its yellow flowers are unusual not only in their appearance—with petals somewhat resembling the legs of a spider—but also in their timing, opening just before the leaves fall in late October. Witch-hazel can be found growing on the high dunes with Black Oak and Penn Sedge and in the shade of Sugar Maple in rich, mesic woods not far from the shores of Lake Michigan. Its small, shiny, black seeds are favorites of songbirds. The similar Spring-flowering Witch-hazel *(H. vernalis)* is native to the south-central United States, including Arkansas, Texas, and Alabama.

CULTURE Witch-hazel is not for every site: Its low branches are most attractive if given room to spread; its leaves require protection from full sun or they scald, turning an unattractive brown; and it cannot tolerate alkaline soil. It prefers moist, well-drained, slightly acidic soil and partial shade. It tolerates average soil moisture but not dry sites. Witch-hazel has a moderate growth rate and is best transplanted as young plants; large plants are slow to become established. If a more upright growth habit is preferred, prune in late autumn or winter after the flowers have faded and the branching structure is revealed. Witch-hazel has few serious insect or disease problems.

COMMON NAME	**BLACK TUPELO**
BOTANICAL NAME	*Nyssa sylvatica*
Height	30–50'
Spread	20–30'
Habit	Pyramidal in youth; rounded–pyramidal with age
Exposure	Sun to partial shade
Soil moisture	Mesic
Fall color	Yellow/orange/red

Black Tupelo can be found growing in low-lying areas of acidic soils, along with Black Chokeberry and Winterberry Holly. It forms a pyramidal, medium-sized shade tree, with branches that come off the central leader like the spokes on a wagon wheel, giving this tree a characteristic appearance all its own. The narrow, 4-inch-long, ovate leaves are leathery and dark green, with fall color rivaled only by the Sugar Maple. The fleshy, $1/2$-inch, oval fruit on female trees are eaten by many birds and other wildlife.

CULTURE Black Tupelo is quite adaptable to various growing conditions and makes an excellent street tree, but its strong taproot can make transplanting difficult. Proper root pruning of young trees (while they are growing in the nursery) and transplanting in spring (when the trees are still dormant) can alleviate some of this difficulty. Once established, Black Tupelo tolerates drought or flooding. It does equally well in full sun or partial shade but prefers a site protected from the wind and moist, well-drained soil that is slightly acidic, with a pH 5.5 to 6.5. It has a moderate growth rate of about one foot a year. Its cold hardiness depends on an individual tree's provenance. It has no serious insect or disease problems.

COMMON NAME	**HOPHORNBEAM**
BOTANICAL NAME	*Ostrya virginiana*
Height	25–40'
Spread	18–25'
Habit	Pyramidal in youth; rounded with age
Exposure	Sun to shade
Soil moisture	Dry to mesic
Fall color	Yellow

Hophornbeam, like Blue Beech, belongs to the birch family and is a multi-stemmed, low-branched, small- to medium-sized tree that can be found growing in the shade of large oaks and Sugar Maples alongside streams. Hophornbeam, however, can also be found in more upland conditions, where soil moisture is not as abundant and soil pH may be more alkaline. Its 2-inch-long, elliptic leaves are similar to those of Blue Beech. It has a somewhat ornamental, vertically striated, gray bark and 2-inch-long, pendulous fruit consisting of papery sacs that overlap like fish scales. Hophornbeam gets its name from these hoplike fruit and from its dense, horn-hard wood.

CULTURE Use Hophornbeam as you would Blue Beech, but it can be used on drier sites. It has an attractive, horizontal branching pattern and when grown in partial shade a more open, pyramidal crown, becoming more broad–rounded and dense in full sun. It has a moderately slow growth rate and can be difficult to transplant. Once established, it can grow up to a foot a year. Multi-stemmed specimens have a more attractive form and stay shorter, about 25 to 30 feet, than those with a single, central leader. It has no serious insect or disease problems.

COMMON NAME	**EASTERN WHITE PINE**
BOTANICAL NAME	*Pinus strobus*
Height	50–80'
Spread	20–40'
Habit	Pyramidal in youth; flattopped with age
Exposure	Sun to partial shade
Soil moisture	Dry to mesic
Fall color	Evergreen

At one time, Eastern White Pine dominated the sand dunes around Lake Michigan in Illinois and Indiana, growing in association with such plants as White, Black, and Chinkapin Oak; Red Osier Dogwood; New Jersey Tea; Little Bluestem; Waukegan Creeping Juniper; and Blue Beech. Most old stands of White Pine were lost to timber harvests in the nineteenth century and subsequent development of the shoreline since that time. Eastern White Pine is not only a good timber tree but also a good choice for the home landscape. This pine is often overlooked in favor of the stiffly conical Norway Spruce and Colorado Spruce. This preference is unfortunate because, rather than becoming an oversized Christmas tree dominating the landscape, White Pine only gets better with age, forming a picturesque, airy tree, naturally limbing itself up and framing, rather than blocking, a house. Its branches radiate from a central leader in distinct, horizontal tiers. The 2- to 4-inch, blue–green needles give each tier a soft, almost cloudlike appearance. White Pine is a good choice for even a small yard and is nice planted with oaks, Quaking Aspen, or Redbud.

CULTURE Eastern White Pine is adaptable to a relatively wide range of growing conditions, but a tree's provenance is important to what the individual tree can tolerate. White Pine grows in very moist to fairly dry, silty clay to sandy soil, in full sun or partial shade. It does not, however, tolerate compacted soils, such as those found around many newly built houses. The needles of Eastern White Pine yellow in high-pH soils, and it does not tolerate road salt on its needles. A nursery-grown tree can be transplanted easily in spring or fall, and a young tree can grow up to 4 feet a year. Guy Sternberg, coauthor with Jim Wilson of *Landscaping with Native Trees*, considers this tree to be one of the most trouble-free pines.

COMMON NAME	**QUAKING ASPEN**
BOTANICAL NAME	*Populus tremuloides*
Height	40–50'
Spread	20–30'
Habit	Pyramidal
Exposure	Sun
Soil moisture	Mesic
Fall color	Yellow

Quaking Aspen is often associated with the Rocky Mountains of Colorado, where vast stands compete for space with Douglas Fir and Ponderosa Pine; but aspen is a widespread species and can be found growing throughout the tallgrass prairie region. Aspen is a pioneer species, often taking hold in open, disturbed sites, where prairie or woodland once occurred. It forms a colony of trees from a common, spreading root system. Young trees have attractive, smooth, light gray, birchlike bark. The 2-inch-wide, heart-shaped leaves, a lustrous dark green above and light gray below, rustle in the lightest breeze and turn a golden yellow in autumn. Aspen is a terrific wildlife tree; birds, butterflies, and small mammals all use the tree in some way.

CULTURE Quaking Aspen grows in just about any soil in full sun. Due to its widespread distribution, a particular tree's regional provenance is important in determining its cultural tolerances. Something else to consider is that female trees produce airborne, cottony seed masses that can cause problems with air-conditioning units and produce seedlings far from the parent plant. These potential problems are easily avoided by choosing a male (and thus seedless) tree. Aspens look best when their clonal, colony-forming tendency is encouraged by allowing several saplings, spaced about 3 to 4 feet apart, to develop into a grove of small trees. After several years, begin to cut out the older stems, as they tend to age poorly, thereby allowing vigorous, light gray, smooth-stemmed sprouts to take their place. Due to its shared root system and easily damaged new bark, the young, fast-growing aspens are best introduced as root cuttings. Aspens produce a light shade, but the shallow, competitive root system makes it difficult for other plants to take hold under its branches. Keep a layer of mulch under aspens to conserve soil moisture and to protect the delicate, young bark from mower damage.

BIG-TOOTHED ASPEN, *Populus grandidentata*
Big-toothed Aspen is similar to Quaking Aspen in character and cultural requirements and is sometimes the prevalent species in prairie regions, such as northern Illinois. Although not as readily available commercially as Quaking Aspen, Big-toothed Aspen can be a more durable choice in such climates.

COMMON NAME	**WHITE OAK**
BOTANICAL NAME	*Quercus alba*
Height	100'
Spread	50–80'
Habit	Broad–rounded
Exposure	Sun
Soil moisture	Mesic to dry
Fall color	Red/brown

White Oak, a potentially large shade tree, is frequently found in dry and mesic woods, often growing in association with Red Oak or Black Oak. Its leaf, on average, is 6 inches long and 3 inches wide, with five to seven rounded lobes and a good crimson red in autumn. The tree generally grows with a straight, central leader and grows straight up, rather than out, if in a confined space. White Oak is a good choice for dry sites.

CULTURE White Oak needs a sunny site with a well-drained soil having a neutral to acidic pH, preferably 5.5 to 6.5. Its leaves yellow in more alkaline sites, and it does not tolerate flood-prone or poorly drained soils. The potential difficulty of transplanting a White Oak is greatly reduced if its taproot was properly root pruned when growing in the nursery. Although oaks are thought to be slow growers, a young White Oak can grow more than a foot a year for its first 20 years. White Oak is susceptible to a number of insect and disease problems but is generally not seriously bothered. To reduce any possible infections carried by insects or the wind, it is best to prune White Oak, if necessary, in winter or early spring.

TREES AND CONSTRUCTION

Most trees, especially White Oaks, are sensitive to soil compaction; and many otherwise salvageable, mature White Oaks are killed during construction of new houses by thoughtless compaction of the soil around their roots, effectively cutting off their air and water supply. This situation can be avoided by installing a temporary but sturdy fence around the drip line of all desirable trees on the property, with signs posted to ensure that no vehicles park under their shade or drive over their roots during construction. Before any construction begins, a certified arborist should be consulted when tree preservation is a concern.

COMMON NAME	**SWAMP WHITE OAK**
BOTANICAL NAME	*Quercus bicolor*
Height	50–60'
Spread	50–60'
Habit	Rounded to broad–rounded
Exposure	Sun to partial sun
Soil moisture	Mesic to wet
Fall color	Yellow/brown

Swamp White Oak forms a medium to large shade tree. It can be found growing in floodplains and other poorly drained sites along with Elderberry. Its leaf is somewhat similar to that of White Oak and is sometimes mistaken for it, but the lobes of Swamp White Oak are less deeply cut. In addition, its young branches have papery, exfoliating bark, a characteristic absent in White Oak.

CULTURE Swamp White Oak's fibrous root system makes it one of the easiest oaks to transplant successfully, as well as allowing it to become established more quickly in a new site. It requires a slightly acidic soil similar to what White Oak requires. Unlike White Oak, Swamp White Oak, as its name implies, grows well in poorly drained soil. Once established, this tree is also quite drought-tolerant, and it does equally well in soils with average soil moisture and good drainage.

COMMON NAME	**SHINGLE OAK**
BOTANICAL NAME	*Quercus imbricaria*
Height	50–60'
Spread	40–50'
Habit	Oval
Exposure	Sun to partial sun
Soil moisture	Mesic
Fall color	Red/brown

Shingle Oak received its name in the eighteenth century from the French colonists who settled the Kaskaskia River Valley in what was to become Illinois. They found that the straight wood grain of this tree allowed it to be split into thin shingles for their new homes. Shingle Oak's native range covers most of the central Midwest, and it can be found growing in moist soils along streams, as well as in drier, upland woods. It has a particularly straight, central leader that remains unforked for the first 20 to 30 feet of growth, giving it a less-spreading crown than many other oaks. Shingle Oak's lustrous, dark green leaves are also quite distinctive among oaks in that they are oblong and unlobed, somewhat like the leaf of a Southern Live Oak *(Quercus virginiana)*. These leaves turn a russet brown in autumn and persist through the winter, providing an effective wind screen.

CULTURE Shingle Oak likes full sun and moist, rich, well-drained soil with an acidic pH but tolerates drier soils and urban conditions well. It transplants moderately well, has a growth rate of about one to 1¹/₂ feet a year. With maturity, trees may require pruning to remove small, lower branches that are shaded out. It rarely shows signs of insect or disease problems.

COMMON NAME	BUR OAK
BOTANICAL NAME	*Quercus macrocarpa*
Height	70–80'
Spread	70–90'
Habit	Broad–rounded
Exposure	Sun
Soil moisture	Mesic to dry
Fall color	Yellow/brown

This low-branched, wide-spreading oak—with its 7-inch, fiddle-shaped leaves and its acorns with heavily fringed caps resembling a large bur—is found on dry, upland ridges as well as moist floodplains. On upland sites, Bur Oaks are widely spaced due to root competition for available soil moisture. These deep and wide-spreading roots, along with the thick, corky bark helped Bur Oak survive the harsh conditions it encountered, including sporadic prairie fires, on the vast, open prairie where few other trees could gain a foothold. These tough, adaptive traits also make it a good tree for urban conditions.

CULTURE Bur Oak is adaptable to a wide range of growing conditions. It requires full sun and prefers moist, slightly alkaline soils; but it does well even in relatively dry, clay soils. It has a moderate growth rate of about one foot a year. Bur Oaks can be difficult to transplant successfully if not properly root-pruned while growing in the nursery.

Although Bur Oak is a potentially large tree, Chicago's Graceland Cemetery (designed by landscape architect O. C. Simmonds at the turn of the twentieth century) has five newly planted Bur Oaks all within the space of 100 square feet—demonstrating that the most creative landscapes require some rules to be broken, chances with failure taken, and foresight exercised.

COMMON NAME	CHINKAPIN OAK
BOTANICAL NAME	*Quercus muehlenbergii [Q. muhlenbergii]*
Height	40–50'
Spread	50–80'
Habit	Open–rounded
Exposure	Sun
Soil moisture	Dry to mesic
Fall color	Yellow/orange

Chinkapin Oak can be found in dry, upland sites, often in alkaline soils along with Sugar Maple, Penn Sedge, Blue Beech, Hophornbeam, and Blackhaw Viburnum; and where the soil is particularly alkaline, with Blue Ash. It can also be found on sand dunes with Witch-hazel. It often grows up to 20 feet before its trunk forks, giving it a vase-shaped branching pattern with an open, rounded crown. Its 8-inch leaves are oblong and coarsely toothed. They hang pendulously from its branches and flutter in the slightest breeze, the dark green upper surface contrasting with a much lighter underside.

CULTURE Because Chinkapin Oak is often found growing in alkaline soil, it is known as a lime-indicator tree and is a good choice for the high-pH soils often found around new housing sites in the upper Midwest. It is adaptable to a wide range of soil conditions, is relatively fast-growing, and is drought-tolerant once established. It has a large taproot and therefore needs to be properly root-pruned in the nursery to help ensure a transplant's success.

SCARLET OAK, *Quercus coccinea*
Like Chinkapin Oak, Scarlet Oak does well in alkaline soils. Growing to a height of 50 to 60 feet, it is similar in appearance to Pin Oak *(Quercus palustris)*, with its pyramidal habit and deeply cut, bristly tipped leaves. But Pin Oak is intolerant of alkaline soils, becoming chlorotic, with the associated yellowing of its leaves. Scarlet Oak is an adaptable, moderately fast-growing tree that can be found growing in moist lowland as well a dry, upland woods, in clay as well as sandy soil. It takes limey soils in stride, showing no signs of yellowed, chlorotic leaves. The very similar Hill's Oak, *Q. ellipsoidalis*, native to the upper Midwest, is sometimes grouped under *Q. coccinea* and has the same attributes.

COMMON NAME	RED OAK
BOTANICAL NAME	*Quercus rubra*
Height	60–75'
Spread	60–75'
Habit	Rounded
Exposure	Sun
Soil moisture	Mesic
Fall color	Orange/red

Red Oak is commonly found growing in rich, mesic woods, alongside White Oak, Sugar Maple, and Hophornbeam. Although Red Oak is similar in growth habit to White Oak, its lobed leaves are bristly tipped, and its bark is dark gray and ridged, in contrast to White Oak's rounded lobes and light gray, platy bark. Because of its beautiful form, cultural adaptability, and relatively fast growth rate, Red Oak has become one of the most commonly planted oaks in the United States and northern Europe.
CULTURE Red Oak's reduced taproot allows it to be transplanted with relative ease, and it has a growth rate of up to 2 feet a year in moist, well-drained soil. It does not do well in alkaline soils but can tolerate urban air pollution and some exposure to road salt. Red Oak recovers more quickly if transplanted in early spring. It has few insect or disease problems in the landscape.

BLACK OAK, *Quercus velutina*
Black Oak and Red Oak are often mistaken for one another, due to their similar size, ridged bark, pointed leaf tips, and habitat preferences. Black Oak, however, differs from Red Oak in that its leaves are more deeply lobed and up to 10 inches long, and its growth habit is pyramidial, with branches angled upward. Black Oak is not often seen for sale in nurseries, but it is an adaptable tree that can be found growing in low, sandy soils or in rocky, well-drained, glacial ridges and clay hillsides. It grows best in moist, acidic, well-drained soils.

COMMON NAME	**STAGHORN SUMAC**
BOTANICAL NAME	*Rhus typhina*
Height	8–25'
Spread	10–20'
Bloom time	Late spring
Flower	4–8", greenish yellow panicle
Exposure	Sun
Soil moisture	Mesic to dry
Fall color	Yellow/orange/red

Staghorn Sumac can be found growing in colonies along woodland edges, where forest gives way to prairie. It forms a small, flattopped tree with a coarse, candelabra- or antlerlike branching pattern. These young branches are covered in a soft, cocoa brown pubescence not unlike the felt on a deer's antlers, hence its common name. By midsummer, the tips of many of the branches are topped by equally pubescent, pointed clusters of red fruit—an interesting and attractive display on the female plants that persists through the winter months. The pinnately divided, fernlike foliage turns beautiful shades of red, orange, and yellow in autumn. For a stunning effect, plant Staghorn Sumac on a low berm, along with prairie wildflowers and grasses. **CULTURE** Staghorn Sumac likes full sun and well-drained soil but is tolerant of a wide range of soil conditions, from sandy to clay, moist to dry. Grown as a single specimen tree in full sun, it forms a picturesque tree 8 to 12 feet tall, sometimes up to 25 feet in a setting where it needs to reach for the sun or where the soil is especially rich and moist. Staghorn Sumac is tolerant of city conditions and dry, sterile soil. It has few insect or disease problems and it is generally a carefree plant. However, if its thin bark is damaged by being hit with a mower or chewed by rabbits, it becomes more susceptible to borer damage and canker development.

CUTLEAF STAGHORN SUMAC, *Rhus typhina* 'Laciniata'
The Cutleaf Staghorn Sumac is a female selection from the East Coast and was chosen for its finely divided leaves, good fruit production, and excellent fall color. The most available form of Staghorn Sumac on the market, it does well in urban settings.

SMOOTH SUMAC, *Rhus glabra*
Smooth Sumac is also a great choice for the home landscape and is similar in appearance to Staghorn Sumac although it does not tend to get as tall, with a maximum height of 10 to 15 feet; and it lacks Staghorn's distinctive fuzzy stems. Smooth Sumac also has a female cutleaf form from the East Coast.

COMMON NAME	**EASTERN ARBORVITAE**
BOTANICAL NAME	*Thuja occidentalis*
Height	20–30'
Spread	10–15'
Habit	Oval to broad–pyramidal
Exposure	Sun to partial shade
Soil moisture	Mesic
Fall color	Evergreen

Eastern Arborvitae can be found growing on moist, calcareous slopes and acidic bogs and in sandy soils along the shores of Lake Michigan. Arborvitae's dense, low-branched crown and scalelike, evergreen foliage provide great cover for songbirds, as well as a very effective screen to unwanted views. It also creates an effective background for the winter displays of Red Osier Dogwood or Winterberry Holly, with masses of Little Bluestem and Prairie Dropseed in the foreground.

CULTURE Eastern Arborvitae should be planted where its roots can stay cool and moist. It does well in alkaline soils and tolerates drought conditions once established. Most specimens sold in nurseries are selected cultivars with various growth habits and winter foliage characteristics. The straight species and some cultivars turn a bronzy brown in winter, while other cultivars have been selected for their consistently green winter color. Arborvitae has a moderate growth rate, and its fibrous root system makes it easy to transplant successfully. Deer enjoy browsing on its foliage (as they do most green things).

COMMON NAME	**BLACKHAW VIBURNUM**
BOTANICAL NAME	*Viburnum prunifolium*
Height	12–15'
Spread	8–12'
Bloom time	Midspring
Flower	2", cream cluster
Exposure	Shade to sun
Soil moisture	Dry to mesic
Fall color	Red/yellow/purple

Often found as an understory plant of upland woods, Blackhaw Viburnum can be grown as a small, single-stemmed tree up to 15 feet tall with a horizontal branching habit or as a colony-forming shrub with strongly vertical stems about 8 feet tall. Either way, it provides a good choice to be underplanted with sun- or shade-loving wildflowers, depending on the site's exposure to the sun. In spring, the plant is covered with creamy white flower clusters; and in autumn, the 2-inch, elliptical leaves turn a nice pinkish red to purple. The small, purple fruit is edible and was used in preserves by the pioneers.

CULTURE Blackhaw Viburnum is adaptable to sun or shade in average to dry soils. Take advantage of this plant's tolerance of shade by giving it a northern exposure. It is easily transplanted but grows relatively slowly and never overpowers a landscape. It has no serious disease or insect problems.

BLOODROOT (*Sanguinaria canadensis*)

NATIVE PLANTS IN THE HOME LANDSCAPE

CHAPTER FIVE

Landscape Designs
with Nature in Mind

The term landscaping has come to mean a cosmetic furnishing of the
landscape, a form of interior decoration done outside. Instead of emulating
the natural environment in all of its complexity and stimulating
a positive experience of nature, many gardens today are purely decorative.
In deference to transient lifestyles, tract houses that go up in a month
are landscaped in a day with instant sod lawns and mature trees and shrubs.
The desire for an instant yard has tended to supersede thoughtful, deliberate
plant selection that places value on ecology, fitness, and meaning.

The California Landscape Garden,
MARK FRANCIS AND ANDREAS REIMAN, 1999

Far too many home landscapes are poorly thought out and generic in their design, and very few take their inspiration from the surrounding natural areas. This is unfortunate, for one of the best ways to create an interesting landscape garden—one that attracts songbirds, butterflies, and other wildlife—is to incorporate plants native to the surrounding region and to use accessible natural areas near your home for design cues. That was how the following examples of five possible garden layouts came into being. None of the designs exactly mimics a particular area, nor should it for the home landscape. In fact, the streamside garden in this section was inspired by Turkey Run State Park in west-central Indiana, as well as by Goodenow Grove Nature Preserve in northern Illinois. Even if the idea for a garden is taken from a single location, the resulting design should always be a distillation of the experience rather than an attempt at a literal re-creation.

The following garden designs could be planted as shown but were intentionally laid out so that they could be easily expanded and manipulated to best suit the unique conditions around your own home. The plans, which are oriented so that the primary view faces the bottom of the page, are overlaid with a grid, with each square representing one square foot. The numbered yellow dots indicate the name of the plant represented on the plan. The number in parentheses, found in the plant list after each plant name, indicates the number of plants needed. Some of the gardens—including the prairie, savanna, and duneland gardens—have a large central area, indicated in purple, where wildflowers indicative of that particular ecotype are mixed with an equal number of Little Bluestem plants. These plants were chosen to grow together well as a unit and to evoke the spirit of the prairie in a small area. These plants in the purple areas should be laid out as if planting a checkerboard of one-foot squares, with all the black squares planted in Little Bluestem and all the red squares planted with a wildflower.

Woodland Garden

After what always seems like a long winter, the appearance of woodland wildflowers is a welcome sign that spring has finally arrived and that warmer days are soon to follow. In spring, the forest floor changes weekly, with a succession of blooms and newly emerging plants. The hard-to-miss blooms of Sharp-lobed Hepatica of this garden, sometimes coming up through a cover of snow, signal the beginning of this display, whether in the woods or in your yard. At the same time hepatica is in bloom, from late March to mid-April, the shimmering Penn Sedge is beginning to send out its flower stalks, and the bold straplike leaves of Chicagoua are busy collecting energy from the sun's rays for its early summer blooms, when the plant is surprisingly leafless. When hepatica is finished blooming, Spring Beauty comes on, carpeting the woodland floor (or lawn) with its month-long display of small pink flowers. Likewise, colonies of trilliums begin to appear, flowering weeks after hepatica, along with the deep pink flowers of Eastern Redbud and the blue flowers of Woodland Phlox and Jacob's Ladder.

Although most of the woodland wildflowers put on their showy displays in early to midspring, when air temperatures are moderate, the soil is moist from spring rains, and before

the oaks and other trees have fully leafed out, the woodland shade garden continues to be a place of understated beauty and solace throughout the growing season. The bold, Water Lily–like blue–green leaves of Bloodroot complement the dissected dark green fronds of Christmas Fern and the finely cut Maidenhair Fern. The wispy, light green colony of Penn Sedge creates a foil for the varied textures and forms of the other plants, allowing a place for the eye to rest and acting as a unifying element in the garden.

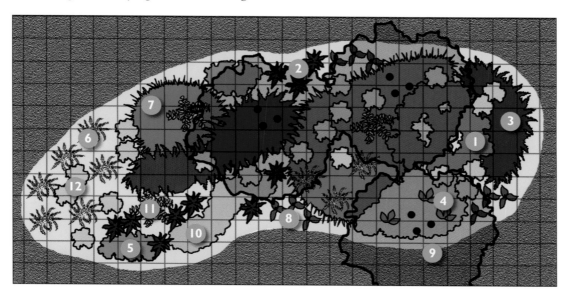

WOODLAND GARDEN PLANTING PLAN

	PLANT LIST					
	Name	**Height**	**Spread**	**Spacing**	**Bloom time**	**Page**
1	Bloodroot (14)	8"	6"	10"	Early spring	42
2	Chicagoua (10)	10"	4"	Random	Early summer	25
3	Christmas Fern (15)	12"	18"	18"	—	50
4	Jack-in-the-Pulpit (3)	12"	8"	Random	Midspring	26
5	Jacob's Ladder (10)	12"	12"	10"	Midspring	39
6	Maidenhair Fern (9)	12"	12"	Random	—	49
7	Penn Sedge (60)	6–8"	8"	6–8"	Early spring	48
8	Prairie Trillium (9)	6–12"	4–8"	Random	Midspring	45
9	Redbud, Eastern (3)	20–30'	25–35'	6'	Early spring	60
10	Sharp-lobed Hepatica (20)	6"	10"	10"	Early spring	33
11	Smooth Solomon's Seal (3)	24"	24"	Random	Mid- to late spring	40
12	Woodland Phlox (18)	12"	10"	Random	Midspring	38

• Although the leaves of Prairie Trillium and Chicagoua disappear from the garden by early summer, others, such as Sharp-lobed Hepatica, Jack-in-the-Pulpit, Smooth Solomon's Seal, and Jacob's Ladder stick around most of the summer, looking good for a longer time if the top 6 to 8 inches of soil are amended with composted organic matter before planting and their roots are kept cool and moist during the growing season with a few inches of wood-chip mulch and supplemental watering during dry summers.

• Three Blackhaw Viburnums or Downy Serviceberries can be substituted for the redbuds; all have similar growth habits and are easily grown in partial shade. Any of these trees would be equally nice in this garden; but for the best springtime display, all three trees should be of the same species. The first two trees have the advantage not only of spring flowers but also of good fall color. Redbuds equal if not surpass the other two in flower and also have nice, heart-shaped leaves during the growing season; but they turn only a poor yellow–green in the fall.

Streamside Garden

The floodplains and slopes along the streams that meander through wooded areas are full of unique and beautiful plants that also do well in the shaded home landscape, with or without an adjacent body of water to complement them. Many of the wildflowers in this garden, including White Trout Lily, Spring Beauty, Virginia Bluebells, and White Trillium are spring ephemerals, going dormant by early summer, not to be seen again until the following spring. However, the remainder, while enjoying moist soil, do not need supplemental watering to do well and provide an effective ornamental display throughout the growing season where a lower-maintenance shade garden is preferred over the more-intensive woodland garden. And

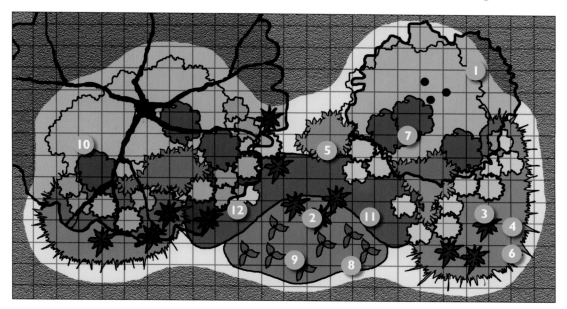

STREAMSIDE GARDEN PLANTING PLAN

PLANT LIST

	Name	Height	Spread	Spacing	Bloom time	Page
1	Blue Beech (1)	20–30'	20–30'	—	Midspring	59
2	Chicagoua (12)	10"	4"	Random	Early summer	25
3	Golden Alexanders (30)	12–36"	12–18"	10"	Mid- to late spring	45
4	Grass Sedge (45)	6"	8"	10"	Midspring	49
5	Great Blue Lobelia (22)	1–3'	12–18"	12"	Late summer into autumn	36
6	Spring Beauty (24)	4–6"	2"	Random	Early spring	29
7	Virginia Bluebells (15)	12"	12"	12"	Early to midspring	37
8	White Trillium (7)	6–12"	4–8"	Random	Midspring	44
9	White Trout Lily (30)	4'	2'	6"	Early spring	30
10	Woodland Geranium (50)	12"	12"	12"	Spring into summer	32
11	Woodland Ginger (40)	6"	Colony	8"	Midspring	26
12	Woodland Phlox (15)	12"	10"	Random	Midspring	38

although its leaves disappear along with the earlier-flowering spring ephemerals, Chicagoua, along with Great Blue Lobelia, provides showy flowers in midsummer.

STREAMSIDE GARDEN: INSTALLATION AND MAINTENANCE NOTES

• Plants in this garden do best in partly shady to shady locations with well-drained soil that has been amended with composted organic matter topped with a few inches of wood-chip mulch or shredded leaves to help conserve soil moisture.

• When provided with the conditions just noted, these plants eventually form colonies of various sizes where lack of competition from other plants allows it. The geraniums fling seed far and wide, as do the Virginia Bluebells, sprouting in any available open ground, and may need to be pulled if they begin to crowd other plants. Spring Beauty, likewise, quickly spreads where open ground allows; because of its small size, however, it generally does not pose a threat to other plants, and the resulting carpet of flowers is quite nice. Great Blue Lobelia is not so aggressive and in fact tends to die out quickly in the face of competition from other more aggressive plants. Also, its evergreen crown of leaves may rot if buried by mulch in winter. Place the White Trilliums where they can be seen and appreciated at close range and given room so that they may eventually spread to form small colonies.

Duneland Garden

In the tallgrass prairie region of the upper Midwest, the dunes along the shores of Lake Michigan contain some of the most varied plant communities, with correspondingly diverse habitats ranging from moist, acidic flatwoods and bogs to dry, sandy dunes and oak savannas. Rather than reflecting any one of these duneland environments, this garden is inspired by the entire duneland region from northeastern Illinois to northern Indiana. The backbone of this garden and what ties it together is the 50:50 mix of sun-loving wildflowers and Little Bluestem. Framing this arrangement are four Red Osier Dogwoods and a single Downy Serviceberry, placed so as not to cast shade on the wildflowers. The lower-growing Prairie Dropseed, Pasture Rose, and Waukegan Creeping Juniper support these taller, central plantings and create a good transition to the lawn area surrounding this garden.

DUNELAND GARDEN: INSTALLATION AND MAINTENANCE NOTES

• This garden looks best, and visual interest is added to the landscape, if it is planted on a slight mound, or berm, of soil to reflect a gently rolling sand dune. So as not to create a distracting and unnatural-looking bump in your home landscape, the berm for this garden plan should be no more than 16 inches high (or about 1 inch of vertical rise in height for every foot of horizontal run in width), creating a slightly level area at its highest point and tapering gradually toward the edge to meet the level of the surrounding lawn.

• A sunny location and average, unamended soil is all that is needed for this garden. If the soil is too rich or consistently moist due to irrigation, the wildflowers may put on so much top growth that they flop over in a storm or when in flower.

• The Pasture Rose and Waukegan Creeping Juniper require pruning to keep them in bounds.

• The dogwoods should have a third of their stems cut back to the ground every year, preferably in early winter. Removing the older stems in this way keeps the plants from becoming overgrown and increases the number of flowers produced in the spring.

• It takes two or three growing seasons for the Prairie Dropseed plants to fill in their space. However, plant spacing should not be reduced to speed this process, as the end result is not as pleasing. Rather, this open space could be filled with well-placed rocks, beach pebbles, and driftwood, allowing the plants to fill in over time.

• After the plants in this garden have become established in their new location, no further watering is necessary or recommended.

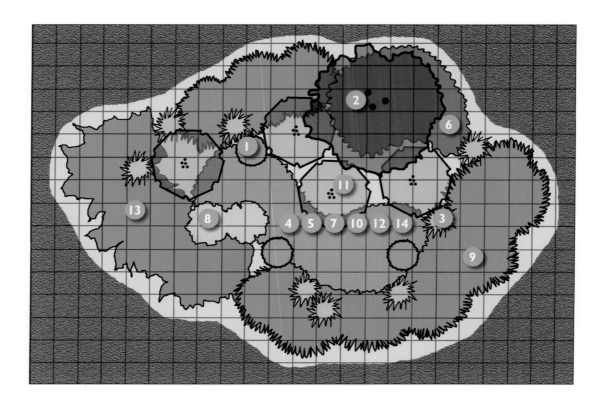

DUNELAND GARDEN PLANTING PLAN

PLANT LIST

	Name	Height	Spread	Spacing	Bloom time	Page
1	Butterfly Milkweed (3)	18–24"	18"	Random	Early summer	27
2	Downy Serviceberry (1)	15–25'	10–12'	—	Early spring	58
3	Dwarf Blazing Star (8)	12–18"	12"	Random	Late summer	35
4	Flowering Spurge (3)	12–36"	8–12"	12"	Early to late summer	31
5	Foxglove Beard Tongue (3)	24"	12"	12"	Early summer	37
6	Kalm's Saint Johns-wort (5)	2–3'	2–3'	18"	Late spring	53
7	Little Bluestem (15)	18–48"	12–18"	12"	Mid- to late summer	46
8	Pasture Rose (2)	1–2'	4–8'	18"	Late spring to midsummer	55
9	Prairie Dropseed (12)	12"	24"	18–24"	Late summer	47
10	Purple Prairie Clover (3)	12–24"	12"	12"	Early to midsummer	38
11	Red Osier Dogwood (4)	4–10'	4–10'	3–6'	Late spring	53
12	Rough Blazing Star (3)	2–5"	12"	12"	Mid- to late summer	34
13	Waukegan Creeping Juniper (3)	6–12'	5–10'	3"	Early spring	54
14	Yellow Coneflower (3)	2–4'	12"	12"	Early summer to autumn	40

Prairie Garden

Prairie gardens are sometimes viewed as eyesores by neighbors with more traditional landscapes. The reason for this perception is often the result of the garden's apparent lack of intent or design. Although many prairie plants are quite beautiful and make great additions to the home landscape, others are best left for larger prairie-restoration projects. With a little planning, a landscape attractive to both neighbor and wildlife can be created. Thought should be given to the ultimate height, growth habits, cultural needs, and ornamental characteristics of each plant. Placing plants so that they complement one another, whether native or exotic, is key to producing a visually pleasing landscape in a small space.

PRAIRIE GARDEN: INSTALLATION AND MAINTENANCE NOTES

• A shortcoming of some prairie gardens is their limited use of grasses and sedges. A prairie garden without a strong presence of grasses and sedges is more reflective of an English perennial border than the great tallgrass prairie. In this design, an evenly distributed mix of Little Bluestem and wildflowers forms the core of the garden. In the spaces between this mix of plants is Penn Sedge. The Penn Sedge adds interest to the early spring garden by forming a

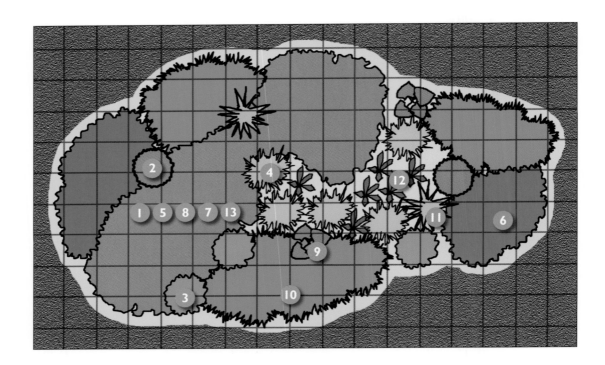

PRAIRIE GARDEN PLANTING PLAN

	Name	Height	Spread	Spacing	Bloom time	Page
	PLANT LIST					
1	Aromatic Aster (6)	24"	18"	12"	Early to midautumn	27
2	Butterfly Milkweed (2)	18–24"	18"	Random	Early summer	27
3	Cream Prairie Indigo (3)	12"	24–30"	Random	Midspring	28
4	Indiangrass (5)	4–5'	24"	Random	Late summer	47
5	Little Bluestem (18)	18–48"	12–18"	12"	Mid- to late summer	46
6	New Jersey Tea (10)	1–3'	3–6'	18"	Late spring to early summer	51
7	Pale Purple Coneflower (6)	2–4'	8"	12"	Early to midsummer	29
8	Penn Sedge (25)	6–8"	8"	6–8"	Early spring	48
9	Prairie Dock (6)	24"	18–24"	10"	Midsummer	42
10	Prairie Dropseed (14)	12"	24"	18–24"	Late summer	47
11	Rattlesnake Master (6)	24"	18"	10"	Midsummer	30
12	Stiff Goldenrod (6)	18"	18"	Random	Early autumn	43
13	Yellow Coneflower (6)	2–4'	12"	12"	Early summer to autumn	40

soft, green carpet from which the other plants emerge. Additionally, bulbs of Spring Beauty can be mixed in, along with the sedge, to heighten the early spring display.

• It takes several growing seasons for the Cream Prairie Indigo and Prairie Dropseed to reach mature size. Be assured, they are stunning when they do. But in the meantime, Black-eyed Susan can be seeded over the open areas; or Hairy Wild Petunia, which spreads to fill the area, can be interplanted among the two until the indigo and dropseed fill their allotted space.

• As with the duneland garden, this garden looks best if it is planted on a slight berm of soil, 12 inches high in the area of the Indiangrass and Stiff Goldenrod, and gently tapering to meet the level of the surrounding grass.

• After the plants in this garden have become established in their new location, no further watering is necessary, or recommended.

Savanna Garden

Unlike the plants in the prairie and duneland gardens (which demand a sunny location) or the woodland garden (where existing shade is necessary for the plants to do well), savanna plants bridge the gap between these two extremes. The wildflowers, grasses, and sedge of this

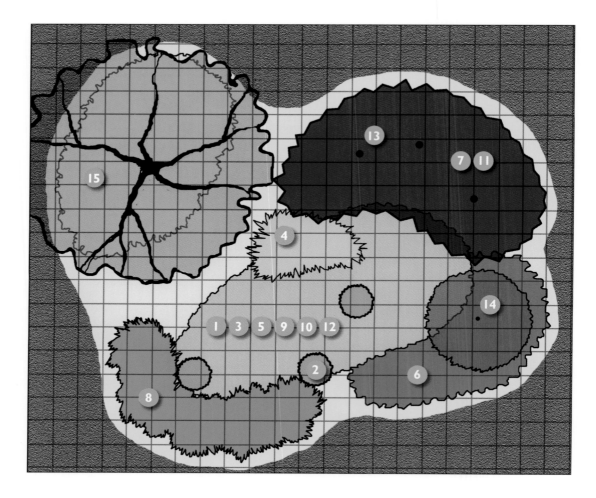

garden can be planted in full sun; but they can also take the dappled shade created as the newly planted oak, surrounded by Woodland Sunflower, reaches maturity. The design of this garden and the choice of plants was inspired by my many visits to Sweetfern Savanna, a Black Oak savanna in the Kankakee River outwash region of northern Illinois.

INSTALLATION AND MAINTENANCE NOTES

• Although often found in the partial shade of oak trees, the plants in this garden are not shade plants. They require at least filtered sunlight for most of the day and even appreciate full sun for part of the day.

• No special soil preparation is needed; as long as the soil is well drained, the plants should grow well.

• As a colony-forming tree, the Staghorn Sumac sends up sprouts, or suckers, from its roots.

PLANT LIST

	Name	Height	Spread	Spacing	Bloom time	Page
1	Black-eyed Susan (6)	12–24"	10"	12"	Late spring to midsummer	41
2	Butterfly Milkweed (3)	18–24"	18"	Random	Early summer	27
3	Flowering Spurge (6)	12–36"	8–12"	12"	Early to late summer	31
4	Indiangrass (8)	4–5'	24"	Random	Late summer	47
5	Little Bluestem (24)	18–48"	12–18"	12"	Mid- to late summer	46
6	New Jersey Tea (10)	1–3'	3–6'	12"	Late spring to early summer	51
7	Penn Sedge (25)	6–8"	8"	6–8"	Early spring	48
8	Prairie Dropseed (7)	12"	24"	18–24"	Late summer	47
9	Purple Prairie Clover (6)	12–24"	12"	12"	Early to midsummer	38
10	Rough Blazing Star (6)	2–5"	10"	12"	Mid- to late summer	34
11	Scarlet Strawberry (15)	6–12"	6–10"	8"	Midspring	31
12	Spiderwort (3)	18–24"	12–18"	12"	Midspring to early summer	44
13	Staghorn Sumac (3)	8–25'	10–20'	3'	Late spring	72
14	White Prairie Indigo (1)	36"	3–5'	—	Late spring	28
15	Woodland Sunflower (40)	24"	Colony	8"	Mid- to late summer	33

These suckers must be removed if space is limited and to keep them from coming up in the mix of wildflowers. They can be easily snapped off at ground level as they appear. The initial planting could start out with two or three small sumacs spaced about 4 feet apart.

• Underplant the sumac with Penn Sedge and Scarlet Strawberry. Both bask in the early spring sun but appreciate the shade cast by the sumac in summer.

• The White Prairie Indigo takes several years to reach mature size, but its display is worth the wait. Its unique beauty and growth habit are showcased best if all but one sprout is removed as they emerge from the ground in midspring. When the indigo is young, however, allowing all the sprouts to come up helps establish an extensive root system more quickly.

• The Woodland Sunflower, which prefers to grow in solid stands, should be separated from the other wildflowers by a narrow walking path. This effectively achieves two goals: Most important, the slight separation keeps the two masses of similar height and form from competing visually; it also allows the spread of the sunflower to be more easily controlled.

• After the plants in this garden have become established in their new location, no further

BLACK-EYED SUSAN (*Rudbeckia hirta*)

NATIVE PLANTS IN THE HOME LANDSCAPE

CHAPTER SIX

Installing and Maintaining
Your Home Landscape

PROPER INSTALLATION AND MAINTENANCE of your new plants are critical for them to grow well and look their best. And although native plants are not very demanding once established in a location, their planting site must be suitably prepared before the plants are installed and properly maintained afterward. Otherwise, the resulting effect is less than hoped for. Disappointment can be avoided by being aware of your plants' needs and providing them a suitable growing environment.

Clearing and Preparing Your Planting Bed

Great, you have chosen the area of your yard where you would like to situate your new planting bed, but now what do you do? One of the first tasks is to eliminate the turfgrass and weeds. There is no right, wrong, or best method for doing this. Rather, you must choose the method that is right for you and your situation.

Herbicides The first and easiest method that may come to mind is the use of a nonselective herbicide, something to kill both grasses and broadleaf weeds such as dandelions. Although spraying an area with a herbicide can be a quick, safe, and effective way of killing unwanted vegetation, there are many types of herbicides on the market, some of which can leach into the soil and stay there, making the area unplantable for long periods, or otherwise be so caustic that they should be applied only by properly trained professionals. If you decide to use a herbicide to get rid of your lawn, choose one that is nonpersistent and marketed for use by homeowners, such as a glyphosate-based product (for example, Roundup or Shootout), and always read the label and follow the manufacturer's instructions. Glyphosate-based herbicides are often used in prairie-restoration work to kill woody and herbaceous weeds. They are readily available at most garden centers, have low toxicity, and break down quickly so that planting can proceed as soon as the weeds are dead (generally in about 2 weeks). Repeated applications or hand-pulling may be necessary to get rid of some of the more persistent weeds.

Other methods of ridding the area of unwanted grass and weeds involve smothering them with an assortment of materials, such as the following:

Leaves In autumn, mark the perimeter of your intended planting bed. Rake a pile of leaves 6 to 12 inches deep into this area and forget about it. The following spring, after you remove the leaves down to a 2-inch layer, the bed is ready for planting. The leaves left intact act as a mulch through which prairie grass and wildflower seedlings can be planted directly. If planting woodland flowers, rake away all the leaves applied in autumn, dig compost into the planting bed as needed, and reapply a 2-inch layer of leaves before planting.

The 6- to 12-inch layer of leaves generally mats down considerably and stays where you put it. However, in some instances, a perimeter of 12-inch chicken-wire fencing may be necessary to help contain the leaves—a consideration if using this method in an open, windy area or near the property line of a neighbor.

Wood chips A 4- to 6-inch layer of wood chips can be used in place of the leaves, as outlined in the preceding method. A distinct advantage to using wood chips is they are available any time of year and are often offered free of charge by many municipalities to their residents. Wood chips may also be an aesthetically more attractive alternative in certain high-visibility areas. Some weeds with extensive taproots, such as dandelions, can be expected to pop up through the mulch, but most are smothered.

Newspaper and wood chips For more immediate results, you can mow your lawn as short as possible, lay down four to six layers of newspaper, wetting them as you go to keep them from blowing away; then cover the area with 2 inches of wood chips. You can plant through the newspaper-and-wood-chip mulch immediately. Using wood chips that have had a chance to compost slightly for a few months is preferable to using fresh wood chips, but either material works well.

Old carpeting, plywood, or black plastic These materials, as well as a variety of others that might be found in your garage or basement, can be laid over an area of lawn where you want your planting bed. Applied in the spring or early summer and left in place throughout the growing season, these materials eventually smother the grass and weeds beneath them, allowing you to plant in autumn (or the following spring) once they have been removed and discarded.

Physically removing the turf and weeds, whether dead or alive, is never necessary (and a lot of work besides!). If adding compost to the soil in preparation of a woodland garden, you can dig the dead turf and weeds into the soil along with the compost; the fine leaves and stems rot quickly, enriching the soil even more. Additionally, if your planting area is on a slope, it is important to leave the dead or soon-to-be-dead plant material in place. While your plantings establish themselves, it keeps the soil stabilized, preventing it from washing away during a rainstorm.

NATIVE PLANTS IN THE HOME LANDSCAPE

When to Plant

WILDFLOWERS AND GRASSES

Spring is the best time to plant your landscape. It is the time of year when the best quality and widest variety of plants are available from garden centers, mail-order catalogs, and local conservation-minded groups that hold annual native plant sales. Most prairie grasses and wildflowers are warm-season species that put on most of their growth when the moist spring soils begin to warm up but the air temperatures are moderate. Thus transplants set out in the spring become established more quickly than if they were planted later in the season. Be aware, however, that new transplants put most of their energy into root growth (rather than top growth) their first season after planting.

Fall planting of grasses and wildflowers is not suggested for a number of reasons. Selection is generally limited to plants that have not sold during the past growing season. The plants that are available may be root-bound in their pots, often making them more difficult to transplant with success. Additionally, the cool soils of fall do not promote vigorous root growth. In fact, the plants may not put out new roots until the following spring, when soils become warm enough to stimulate growth. Without extensive roots to anchor them, the plants are likely to be pushed out of the ground as the soil freezes and thaws repeatedly throughout the winter. This upheaval exposes the crown of the plant, where most new growth arises, to dry winter winds, leaving little chance for new growth to appear in the spring. If you decide to plant in the fall, you can reduce the likelihood of the plants' heaving out of the ground by covering the newly installed plants with 4 to 6 inches of leaf or straw mulch after the ground freezes in late autumn. This layer of insulation helps keep the ground frozen throughout the winter, thus reducing the likelihood that the plants are pushed out of the ground.

There is, however, one advantage of fall planting over spring planting: Plants bought in the fall are often greatly reduced in price. If the plants available are ones you would like to grow, then fall planting may be worth the risk of losing a few of them over the winter.

TREES AND SHRUBS

Spring is also the best time to plant deciduous trees and shrubs because both produce maximum root growth in early summer, and the odds of successful transplanting are increased if they are planted during this period of active growth. Fall planting is less successful because the newly planted trees and shrubs often become desiccated due to dry winds and frozen soil. For these reasons, plant nurseries dig a majority of their stock out of their fields in early spring. By planting these balled-and-burlapped (B&B) trees and shrubs in your yard soon after they are dug and still in winter dormancy, you will find that the plants show fewer signs of transplant stress—as indicated by slow growth and reduced vigor—and become established in their new sites more quickly than if planted in full leaf in the hotter, drier conditions later in the season. Conifers, such as White Pine, however, have more uniform root growth throughout the growing season, and the time of transplanting is not as critical. Container-grown trees and shrubs, likewise, can be planted just about any time of year and are a better choice for midsummer planting over field-grown B&B stock.

Mulching Your Plants

Mulch is any organic material, such as wood chips or shredded leaves, applied to the surface of the soil in a layer 2 to 4 inches deep around plantings. Mulch is primarily used to conserve soil moisture and to help keep weeds from coming up in the planting beds. But mulch has many other benefits as well, such as moderating soil temperatures, which can vary greatly between hot days to cool nights, increasing the organic content and thus the water-holding capacity of the soil, providing easily damaged tree trunks a ring of protection from weed-eaters and mowers, reducing soil erosion, and generally improving the overall appearance of the planting bed. However, if mulch is misapplied, it can have negative effects as well.

If mulch is used on poorly drained soil, it can keep the soil excessively moist, potentially drowning the roots of the plant. Similarly, if mulch is applied too thickly (more than 5 inches deep), gas exchange between the air and soil is reduced to the point of causing plant death by suffocation. A layer of mulch needs to be only 3 or 4 inches deep over the roots of a tree or shrub to be effective, and it should never be mounded around the trunk of a tree or shrub. The moisture held by the mulch against the plant tissue can cause stems and tree trunks to rot or open them up to potential damage by insects, fungi, or rodents, such as voles, moles, or mice (nesting in the mulch because it was applied incorrectly). There should always be a mulch-free zone of a few inches around the trunk of a tree or the base of any other plant.

A few things to keep in mind when using mulch:

• For optimal root growth, spread mulch no deeper than 3 or 4 inches around shrubs and trees. If mulch is any deeper, anaerobic conditions can be created at the soil line, starving the roots of air.

• Always keep mulch 1 or 2 inches away from the base of a plant. Never pile mulch like a volcano around trees or any other plant. This practice can damage plant tissue, as well as direct much needed water away from the root ball.

• To encourage new root growth, create a mulch ring around newly installed trees three times the diameter of the root ball (figure 6.1, page 95).

• Native wildflowers and grasses should be mulched to a depth of 1 or 2 inches. Any deeper can cause the crowns of the plants to rot.

• After the first year, native grasses and wildflowers do well without mulch, but its use improves the appearance of the planting beds.

• Add additional mulch around plants every 2 or 3 years as needed.

Watering

Irrigating, or watering, your native plants—beyond what the rain clouds provide—is not necessary once they become established in their new location. For prairie grasses and wildflowers, you need to water your plants only during the first growing season and then only when the surface of the soil is dry beneath the mulch. Watering after the first year is not necessary and in fact may cause the plants to put on so much top growth that they flop over. The sun-loving grasses and wildflowers chosen for this book all prefer well-drained soils with average to poor fertility and are able to withstand drought conditions. However, during periods of drought—less than one inch of rain in one month's time or no rain for 3 weeks—watering your prairie garden can extend the flowering period of the plants, but it is not necessary for their survival. The woodland wildflowers are another story: Although they do fine with average soil moisture and no additional watering, they look better (and for a longer period) if soil moisture is consistent throughout the growing season. This can be accomplished by ensuring that an adequate amount of organic matter is added to the soil before planting, keeping the plants mulched with shredded leaves or wood chips, and supplemental watering during dry summers.

Newly planted trees may need several years of irrigation until they have sent out enough roots to replace the ones lost when being dug from the nursery field. Until the roots are reestablished, the newly planted tree puts out very little if any new top growth and needs supplemental watering just to maintain its leaf canopy.

A tree's size, and hence its price, is determined by measuring the width of its trunk, or caliper, about 6 inches above the soil line. Generally, a tree needs one year for every inch of trunk caliper to replace the roots it lost when it was dug from the growing field. Therefore, a tree of larger caliper needs several years of supplemental watering while its root mass is trying to catch up with its existing top growth. Illinois nurseryman Connor Shaw observed that a 1.75-inch-caliper Bur Oak that he planted in his backyard grew 8 feet in 4 years, while a 3.5-inch-caliper Bur Oak planted nearby grew only 8 inches in the same time due to its slower recovery period. Pruning to reduce the crown of the tree to balance the reduced root mass, however, does not help recovery time; it merely reduces the ability of the tree to produce the energy it needs for root growth.

The Planting and Care of New Trees (and Shrubs)

As mentioned, early spring is the best time to plant new trees. However, *how* you plant a tree is equally as critical as *when* you plant it. Observing the following guidelines can increase the chances that your newly planted tree establishes itself quickly and grows vigorously in its new site.

Have your underground utility lines marked. Before digging in your yard, you should always call to have these lines marked so that you can avoid them. This free service is provided by the utility companies. You can find the phone number to call on your utility bill or in the front of the phone directory.

Choose the right tree for the site. Consider the site's exposure to dry winter winds and how much sun or shade it receives. Determine how well the soil drains and whether the soil is generally wet, dry, or in between. Check the soil for compaction, as well as pH. Also take into account the presence of overhead utility wires. Avoid having your tree "pruned" by the utility company by planting potentially large trees far from these lines.

Dig a proper hole for the tree. Measure the width and height of the root ball with a tape measure or yardstick. Dig a hole three times the width of the root ball and 2 inches shallower than the height of the root ball (figure 6.1, page 95). Most of a tree's roots are in the top 6 to 12 inches of soil, not deep in the ground. By digging a wide hole, you loosen the soil where most of the roots grow, and you eliminate competition for water from existing turfgrass or weeds. This procedure is especially important around new buildings, in urban settings, and in clay soils where soil compaction is often an issue. By making the hole a bit shallower than the height of the root ball, you can set the tree just slightly above the existing level of the soil. This practice keeps the root flare (where roots meet the trunk) of the tree from being buried, as well as helps to ensure good drainage—both important considerations for the health of the tree.

Double-check the depth of the hole before setting in the tree. Once a tree is set into a planting hole that is too deep, getting soil under the root ball to raise it is difficult. Even more important, the young feeder roots could be seriously damaged while jostling the tree in the process or while attempting to lift the tree out of the hole. Before you set the tree into its planting hole, it is always wise to double-, triple-, or even quadruple-check the depth of the root ball against the depth of the hole. If the hole is too deep, add soil to the hole and compact it as much as possible so that it does not settle. Keep in mind that the roots of the tree grow out not down. Loose soil at the bottom of the hole is of no benefit to the tree. It can in fact be detrimental to the health of the tree if its settlement causes the tree's trunk flare to sink below the soil line, which shortens the life of the tree.

Backfill the hole gently but firmly. Only after the tree is positioned should you start backfilling the hole. Begin by filling the hole one-third full, gently tamping the soil as you fill to help stabilize the tree and to avoid creating large air pockets. (Tree roots stop growing when they encounter large air pockets.) Running water at a gentle trickle into the hole as you fill it with soil also helps settle the soil around the root ball. At this time, you can cut away the string or wire from the top half of the root ball and the trunk of the tree. Also, cut away the burlap from the top one-third of the root ball or remove it entirely if the root ball is wrapped in synthetic burlap. Any burlap left exposed to the air after planting wicks moisture away from the root ball. Continue adding soil and tamping until the hole is full. Mound the leftover soil around the edge of the planting hole to direct water to the roots, but remove this lip after the first season to encourage roots to grow beyond this area of optimal moisture.

Mulch the tree properly. It is important to keep your newly planted tree properly mulched (see page 92; figure 6.1, page 95). Mulch helps to insulate the ground, keeps the soil evenly moist, eliminates weed and grass competition, and keeps weed-eaters and lawn mowers away from the easily damaged bark of the young tree.

Water the tree properly. (See page 93.) Until the tree becomes established in its new location, water it thoroughly at least once a week (letting the hose run for half an hour at a steady

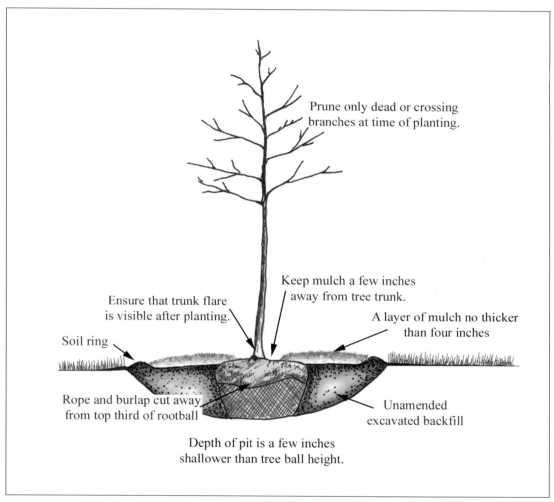

Prune only dead or crossing branches at time of planting.

Keep mulch a few inches away from tree trunk.

Ensure that trunk flare is visible after planting.

A layer of mulch no thicker than four inches

Soil ring

Rope and burlap cut away from top third of rootball

Unamended excavated backfill

Depth of pit is a few inches shallower than tree ball height.

Figure 6.1 TYPICAL TREE PIT, BASED ON THE INTERNATIONAL SOCIETY OF ARBORICULTURE'S *TREE PLANTING GUIDELINES* AND *URBAN SOIL IN LANDSCAPE DESIGN* BY PHILLIP J. CRAUL (1992)

trickle) or anytime the soil of the root ball is dry under the mulch. Following this procedure keeps the soil moist but not wet. Continually wet soil can starve a tree's roots of needed air, causing the leaves to yellow and fall from the tree.

A few things to keep in mind when planting a tree:

Handle the tree only by its root ball. Never drag or lift a tree by its trunk or use the tree's trunk as a lever when attempting to adjust it in its hole. Doing so damages the tree's fine feeder roots.

Limit your initial pruning to dead or rubbing branches. Do not remove healthy growth. The young tree needs all its top growth to produce the energy needed to reestablish its root system.

Do not fertilize your tree at the time of planting. Doing this causes the tree to put on more top growth than its roots can support.

Do not wrap the trunk of the tree. Tree wraps can hold moisture, creating an ideal habitat for insects that may damage the bark of the tree; and the string used to hold the wrap in place could kill the tree by girdling it.

Never lift a tree from its container. When planting container-grown trees, always cut away the container or tear it away if the pot is made of peat. If the tree is pulled or lifted from the container by its trunk, the weight of the soil ball damages the roots.

Check the roots of container-grown trees. Container-grown trees often have roots that circle around the outside of the root ball, often becoming so dense that the plant becomes root-bound. The health of the tree can be affected if these encircling roots are not dealt with before planting. The root mass must be slit vertically with a knife or teased loose if possible. Unless this is done, the roots continue to grow in circles (rather than growing out into the soil) when the tree is planted.

Roughen the surface of the planting hole. Trees can become "pot-bound" if the surface of the planting hole is glazed or smeared. This problem can be most severe in holes that are mechanically dug with a tree spade.

Backfill the hole with the soil that came out of it. Never enrich the soil used to fill the hole with compost or other material. Doing so will keep the roots from spreading into the unamended soil surrounding the planting hole. However, former University of Illinois Extension specialist Denny Schrock recommends that "whenever strong soil textural differences exist between the root ball of the tree and the surrounding soil, there may be benefit to soil amendment—on a large scale. Roots don't readily penetrate soil textural differences. So, for example, if a container-grown plant in a highly organic soilless mix is planted in a heavy clay soil, the roots may remain confined to the old root ball. In this case, it may be helpful to provide a gradual transition of soil types from the highly organic container mix to the low-organic clay soils. It is important not to amend just a small area or you end up transplanting the plant into a larger 'pot.' If amendment is necessary, it is best to treat a wide area."

Do not stake a newly planted tree. Properly dug, nursery-grown trees should not require staking for support. The mass of the root ball should be able to support the tree. A properly dug tree has a root ball that is 9 to 12 inches across for every 1 inch of trunk diameter, measured 6 inches above the trunk flare. Additionally, staking a newly planted tree causes its stem to be weaker and its root growth less vigorous. The only time a tree may need to be staked is if it is planted in an area with high winds or where the tree may be subject to abuse by passing pedestrians.

Identify the location of the tree's trunk flare. The trunk flare, the area where the roots meet the trunk, should always be visible after planting. If the trunk flare is buried in the soil ball as it comes from the nursery, remove this excess soil before planting. If, after planting, a tree's trunk flare is buried in either soil or mulch, the tree slowly suffocates—dying in as little as 2 years or existing in a weakened state for many years until some other stress, such as drought, kills it.

Labeling Your Plants

It is always a good idea to mark with a label the location of newly installed transplants. Labels are especially important the first year or two when new plants are being installed because some young grasses and wildflowers are relatively small and easily injured by foot traffic or may be mistaken for weeds. Also, it is easy to forget, even with a planting plan, where everything is located. In the event something fails to come up the following spring, you know what was lost by having it labeled. Additionally, some plants may not be visible during certain parts of the growing season, such as the late-to-emerge Butterfly Milkweed or some of the early flowering woodland wildflowers that go dormant and disappear by midsummer. If these plants are not labeled, you may attempt to plant something on top of them or mistakenly bury them with mulch (which may rot their crowns). If a plant does not come with a label, you can purchase blank labels or—even better—make them easily enough from salvaged household items.

For example, old venetian blinds with 1-inch louvers make great plant labels. Simply take the blind apart and cut the individual louvers into sections 6 to 8 inches long. Use a pencil (ink fades) to write the name of the plant and the date that it was planted.

Another method uses aluminum soda cans. The process involves cutting away the top and bottom of the can with a pair of scissors. Once this is done, cut the remainder of the can into strips about an inch wide and 3 inches long. Make a hole at one end of the strip with a paper hole punch. You can write on the tag by using a ballpoint pen as an embossing tool. To do this, lay the aluminum strip printed side down on a magazine or a piece of belt leather. Then, using the pen, write on the strip as you would a piece of paper. These embossed tags are unobtrusive and never fade. They can be hung from a wire stuck in the ground. Surveyor's flags, the kind used to mark underground utilities, are a good source of stiff wire. If you are labeling a tree or shrub, the label can be tied directly to a branch.

Glossary of Terms

BALLED AND BURLAPPED
Also termed B&B; refers to the root ball of a nursery-grown tree or shrub, dug from the growing field and wrapped in burlap in preparation for sale.

BERM
An elongated mound of soil created to add interest to a landscape or to increase privacy.

BIODIVERSITY
The variety and abundance of life forms found in a particular area.

BIPINNATELY DIVIDED
In reference to a leaf, one in which the main axial vein has secondary veins with attached leaflets coming off of them laterally.

BUNCHGRASS
Grasses in which the leaves arise from a crown rather than spreading rhizomes.

CALIPER
In reference to nursery-grown trees, the diameter, or width, of the trunk of a tree, measured 6 inches above the ground.

CONTAINER-GROWN
Nursery-grown plants that are grown and sold in pots, as opposed to field-grown nursery stock that is balled and burlapped.

CULTIVAR
A cultivated variety; typically, a named plant selection. Many plants have several named cultivars, for example 'Husker Red' Penstemon is a cultivar of *Penstemon digitalis*. Cultivars are selected strains propagated by nurseries for certain hardiness or ornamental characteristics, such as prolonged flowering time. The selected characteristics are maintained by propagation of root or stem cuttings, as well as by tissue culture.

DRIP LINE
The outer limit of a tree's crown of leaves where water would drip after a period of rainfall. It is an area where many fine feeder roots can be found.

FLATWOOD
A low, wooded area not immediately adjacent to a stream or other body of water. These low-lying areas hold water for an extended period after a rainfall due to a layer of clay just below the surface of the soil.

GIRDLE
The action of scoring the bark of a tree all the way around its circumference and through the living cambium layer, effectively cutting off nutrients to the roots of the tree and killing it. Girdling can also be caused by tight constriction, such as a root wrapped around the trunk or other roots.

LEGUME
Plants that belong to the Fabaceae, or pea, family and produce pods for fruit. Examples include Leadplant and the prairie indigos.

MESIC
A term used to describe soil conditions that are neither wet nor dry—but rather, moist and well-drained; conditions that are generally found around most homes.

MULCH
Any organic or inorganic matter laid over the roots of a plant in a thin layer to help conserve soil moisture and reduce weed growth.

MULCH RING
A layer of mulch surrounding an individual tree or shrub.

NATIVE PLANT
For the purposes of this publication, any plant that could be found growing in the Midwest before European settlement of North America.

NITROGEN–FIXING
Nitrogen is an important nutrient needed for leaf and stem production. Most plants can use only forms of nitrogen found in the soil (such as nitrate and ammonium); however, some species, mostly in the pea (legume) family, can make use of pure atmospheric nitrogen. This is accomplished by a

mutually beneficial relationship between the host plant, such as Leadplant or New Jersey Tea, and a specific soilborne bacteria that resides in nodules formed on the roots of the host. The bacteria absorb atmospheric nitrogen and change it to a form that the plant can use; in return, the bacteria absorb nutrients and moisture from the roots of the plant. Each species of nitrogen-fixing bacteria is specific to an individual species of plant; in certain soils, the bacteria may be absent, therefore some nurseries artificially inoculate the plants with the appropriate bacterial species.

POT-BOUND
Many container-grown plants bought later in the growing season have a solid mass of roots circling the inside of the pot. These roots need to be sliced off or vertically slashed with a knife before planting so that the roots can grow out into the soil rather than continuing to circle.

PRAIRIE
Meaning "grazed meadow," the term chosen by seventeenth-century French explorers to describe the seemingly endless expanse of grasses and wildflowers they encountered in central North America.

PROVENANCE
Over long periods, plants become genetically adapted to certain climates and growing conditions; therefore a species, such as Butterfly Milkweed, growing in southwestern Michigan has a different genetic fingerprint, or genotype, than one growing in eastern Iowa or northern Arizona. Because many prairie plants are widespread, it is important to know the source, or provenance, of your plant material to ensure its hardiness in your growing location.

ROOT BALL
The mass of roots and soil of a transplant.

SAVANNA
While a woodland has a leaf canopy that covers more than half of its underlying ground and vegetation, a savanna has a canopy cover of between 10 and 50 percent; and hence its understory vegetation receives much more sunlight. Savannas are generally identified by their major oak constituent; examples include Black Oak savannas and Bur Oak savannas.

SEPAL
Sepals are generally green and make up the calyx or the cuplike part of the flower just below the petals where the stem meets the flower. In the case of Sharp-lobed Hepatica, however, the flowers lack petals, and the showy, petal-like structures are actually its sepals.

SPRING EPHEMERAL
This term refers to woodland plants that emerge, flower, then go dormant, not to be seen until the following spring. Trout Lily, the trilliums, and Spring Beauty are examples.

STRAIGHT SPECIES
Any plant as found in nature that produces similar offspring by seed production without any human selection or intervention is termed a "straight species." The use of cultivars can be helpful to get a particular, desired trait such as better fall color, whereas the use of a straight species can provide a broader genetic base to resist a variety of environmental conditions, diseases, or insects.

TRANSPLANT STRESS
When field-grown trees and shrubs are dug and transplanted to a new location, the plants generally show signs of stress, such as leaf drop, wilted or yellowing foliage, and branch dieback. These conditions are caused by the greatly reduced root mass of the plant. Transplant stress can be lessened by planting field-grown trees and shrubs soon after they are dug, while dormant in early spring or late fall. Proper watering and mulching after planting helps as well. Likewise, removing only dead or crossing branches at planting helps the tree or shrub reestablish its root system more quickly than if a severe pruning is done. Fertilizing a newly planted tree or shrub only adds additional stress by forcing the plant to put on more top growth than the plant's roots can support.

TRUNK FLARE
The area of a tree where the roots meet the trunk (see figure 6.1, page 95).

VARIETY
A naturally occurring group of plants, abbreviated "var." (as in *Crataegus crusgalli* var. *inermis)* and indicating a difference, such as thornlessness, from the straight species, with this difference being passed on to the seeding offspring.

Native Plant Sources

Source list and comments courtesy of the Grand Prairie Friends of Illinois
www.grandprairiefriends.org

Illinois

ART AND LINDA'S WILDFLOWERS
www.artandlindaswildflowers.com
3730 South 59th Avenue
Cicero, IL 60804
(708)863-6534
ArtandLindasWildflowers@hotmail.com
Offers local genotype woodland and prairie plants.

BLAZING STAR NURSERY
www.blazing-star.com
2107 Edgewood Drive
Woodstock, IL 60098
(815)338-4716
tallgrass@blazing-star.com
Offers prairie, savanna, and wetland plants and seeds, consulting.

BLUESTEM PRAIRIE NURSERY
13197 East 13th Road
Hillsboro, IL 62049
(217)532-6344; fax, (217)532-6344
schaal@cillnet.com
Offers local-ecotype prairie seeds and bare-root plants. Free catalog.

COUNTRY ROAD GREENHOUSE
www.prairieplugs.com
19561 East Twombly
Rochelle, IL 6106
(815)384-3311
Offers wholesale prairie and wetland plants.

CURRENTS COMPANY
Route 2, Box 176
Wyoming, IL 61491
(309)286-7366

EARTHSKIN NURSERY
www.earthskinnursery.com
9331 NCR 3800E
Mason City, IL 62664
(217)482-3524
lrnelms@fgi.net
Offers nursery-grown, central Illinois-ecotype prairie seed.

ENDERS GREENHOUSE
104 Enders Drive
Cherry Valley, IL 61016
(815)332-5255
Offers prairie, woodland, and wetland plants.

GENESIS NURSERY
23200 Hurd Road
Tampico, IL 61283
(815)438-2220
Offers northwest Illinois ecotypes of prairie, wetland, and savanna seeds and plants.

GERARD & GREENE NURSERY
www.gerardandgreene.com
Crete, IL
(708)672-1201
Offers south Cook and eastern Will counties ecotype woodland and prairie plants. Native landscape services.

GRAND PRAIRIE FRIENDS
www.grandprairiefriends.org
P.O. Box 36
Urbana, IL 61803
Offers native plants each spring on Mother's Day weekend and at the Urbana Farmers' Market.

LAFAYETTE HOME NURSERY
LaFayette, IL 61449
(309)995-3311
Offers seeds.

LANDSCAPE NATURALLY, INC.
1021 Janet St.
Sycamore, IL 60178
(815)899-7574
*Offers seeds from within 90 miles of
St. Charles, and consulting for prairie
restorations.*

MIDWEST WILDFLOWERS
Box 64
Rockton, IL 61072
*Offers native wildflower seeds, books;
catalog.*

NATIVE PLANT MATERIALS
766 Bateman Street
Galesburg, IL 61401
Offers seeds.

THE NATURAL GARDEN
38 W 443 Highway 64
St. Charles, IL 60174
(630)584-0595
*Offers seeds of prairie grasses and forbes,
perennials, and woodland wildflowers. One
of the largest suppliers in the Chicago area.*

PECASUGAR NURSERY
www.pecasugar.com
13002 Harrison Road
Shirland, IL 61079
(815) 629-2546; fax, (815)629-2546
kwwinters@earthlink.net

POSSIBILITY PLACE NURSERY
www.possibilityplace.com
7548 W. Monee–Manhattan Road
Monee, Illinois 60449
(708)534-3988; fax, (708)534-6272
info@possibilityplace.com
*Offers wholesale and retail trees, shrubs,
grasses, and forbs native to northern Illinois.*

PRAIRIE DOCK NURSERY
2731 County Road 100N
Allerton, IL 61810
(217)834-3146

THE PRAIRIE GARDEN
705 South Kenilworth Avenue
Oak Park, IL 60304
(708)386-7495

THE PRAIRIE PATCH
RR 1, Box 41
Niantic, IL 62551
(217)668-2409

THE PROPAGATORS PRIVATE STOCK
8805 Kemman Road
Hebron, IL 60034
*Offers select perennial, wildflower, and woody
landscape plants.*

Indiana

EARTHLY GOODS, LTD.
www.earthlygoods.com
P.O. Box 614
New Albany, IN 47150

EDGE OF THE PRAIRIE WILDFLOWERS
711 West Pike
Crawfordsville, IN 47933
(765)362-0915

HEARTLAND RESTORATION SERVICES, INC.
www.earthsourceinc.net
349 Airport North Office Park
Ft. Wayne, IN 46825
(219)489-8511; fax, (219)489-8607

NEW, J.F., & ASSOC.
www.jfnew.com
708 Roosevelt Road
P.O. Box 243
Walkerton, IN 46574
(219)586-3400
*Offers northern Indiana–ecotype wetland
and prairie plants and seeds, planting, and
mitigation consulting.*

SPENCE RESTORATION NURSERY
www.spencenursery.com
2220 East Fuson Road
Muncie, IN 47308
(317)286-7154

WOODY WAREHOUSE NURSERY
www.woodywarehouse.com
P.O. Box 259
Lizton, IN 46149
(866)766-8367; fax, (317)944-5494
Offers native deciduous tree seedlings.

Iowa

ALLENDAN SEED
1966 175th Lane
Winterset, IA 50273-8500
(515)462-1241
Iowa-grown native grass.

CEDAR RIVER GARDEN CENTER
P. O. Box 259
2889 Palo Marsh Rd.
Palo, IA 52324-0259
(319) 851-2161; fax, (319)851-2164
Landscape services, native wildflower plants, and seeds.

HEYNE CUSTOM SEED SERVICES
26420 510th Street
Walnut, IA 51577-4110
(800)784-3454; fax, (712)784-2030
heyne@netins.net
Offers custom, native-Iowa seeds and plants, plus services such as planting, harvesting, and seed contitioning.

ION EXCHANGE
www.ionxchange.com
1878 Old Mission Drive
Harpers Ferry, Iowa 52146-7533
(800)291-2143, (319)535-7231; fax, (319)535-7231
hbright@means.net
Offers seeds for forbs, grasses, sedges, and rushes. Also offers an extensive list of books.

IOWA PRAIRIE SEED COMPANY
P.O. Box 228
Sheffield, IA 50475
(515)892-4111
Offers local-ecotype seed.

OSENBAUGH GRASS SEEDS
Route 1, Box 44 Lucas, IA 50151
(800)582-2788; (515)766-6795
Offers consulting and Iowa-ecotype plants and seeds.

PRAIRIE GRASS UNLIMITED
P.O. Box 59
Burlington, IA 52601
(319)754-8839

REEVES WILDFLOWER NURSERY
28431 200th Street
Harper, IA 52231
(641)635-2817

Michigan

MICHIGAN WILDFLOWER FARM
11770 Cutler Road
Portland, MI 48875-9452
(517)647-6010
Offers Michigan native wildflower and grass seed.

NESTA PRAIRIE PERENNIALS
1019 Miller Road
Kalamazoo, MI 49001
(800)233-5025
Offers greenhouse-propagated native perennials and wildflowers. Retail/wholesale plugs.

Minnesota

BOOMING NATIVE PLANTS
2323 County Road 6 East
Barnum, MN 55707
(218)389-3220
Offers local- and Midwest-ecotype wildflower seeds and plants.

FEDER'S PRAIRIE SEED COMPANY
12871 380th Avenue
Blue Earth, MN 56013-9608
(507)526-3049; fax, (507)526-3509
feder@bevcomm.net
Offers local-ecotype seed.

KASTE, INC.
Route 2, Box 153
Fertile, MN 56540
(218)945-6738
Offers varietal grass seed and local-ecotype forb seed.

LANDSCAPE ALTERNATIVES, INC.
www.landscapeaslternatives.com
1705 St. Albans Street
Roseville, MN 55113
(612)488-3142
Offers prairie, wetland, and woodland plants.

MARK E. GULLICKSON
Route 2, Box 150A
Fertile, MN 56540
(218)945-6894
Offers varietal grass seed and local-ecotype wildflower seed.

MOHN SEED COMPANY
Route 1, Box 152
Cottonwood, MN 56229
(507)423-6482
Offers varietals and local ecotypes.

MORNING SKY GREENERY
www.morningskygreenery.com
Route 1, Box 137
Hancock, MN 56244
(320)392-5282; fax, (320)392-5282
mornsky@info-link.net
Offers local-ecotype prairie plants.

NATURALLY WILD ORGANIC WILDFLOWERS AND PERENNIALS
3539 West 44th Street (nursery location)
4712 Drew Avenue South (mailing address)
Minneapolis, MN 55410
(612)922-2468

NORTH AMERICAN PRAIRIES COMPANY
11754 Jarvis Avenue
Annandale, MN 55302
(320)274-5316; fax, (320)274-5316
info@northamericanprairies.com

ORCHID GARDENS
2232 139th Avenue NW
Andover, MN 55304
(612)755-0205
Offers native wildflowers, ferns, and shrubs. Catalog, 50 cents.

OX CART SEED COMPANY
Route 3, Box 226
Hawley, MN 56549
(218)937-5639
Offers varietals, local-ecotype switchgrass and big bluestem.

PRAIRIE HILL WILDFLOWERS
Route 1, Box 19-A
Ellendale, MN 56026
(507)451-7791
Offers local ecotypes of prairie species.

THE PRAIRIE IS MY GARDEN
www.theprairieismygarden.com
13633 Ferman Avenue NW
Clearwater, MN 55320
(612)878-1694; fax, (612)878-1720
information@theprairieismygarden.com

PRAIRIE MOON NURSERY
www.prairiemoonnursery.com
Route 3, Box 163
Winona, MN 55987-95
(507)452-1362
pmnrs@luminet.net
Offers prairie, woodland, and wetland seeds and plants.

PRAIRIE RESTORATIONS, INC.
   www.prairieresto.com
   P.O. Box 327
   Princeton, MN 55371
   (612)389-4342
   prairie@sherbtel.net
   Offers restoration and management; local-genotype prairie seeds and plants.

SHOOTING STAR NATIVE SEEDS
   www.shootingstarnativeseed.com
   P. O. Box 648
   Highway W & County Road 33
   Spring Grove, MN 55974
   (507)498-3944; fax, (507)498-3953
   ssns@means.net
   Offers local-genotype prairie grass and wildflower seeds.

WILDLIFE HABITAT
   RR 3, Box 178
   Owatonna, MN 55060
   Offers grass-seed production.

Missouri

EASYLIVING NATIVE PERENNIAL WILDFLOWERS
   www.easywildflowers.com
   P.O. Box 105913
   Jefferson City, MO 65109
   (573)761-0543
   john@easywildflowers.com

ENVIRONMENTAL REPAIR SERVICES
   www.prairiesource.com
   P.O. Box 152
   Clinton, MO 64735
   (660)885-6127
   ers@prairiesource.com
   Consulting, contracting, Truax seeders, Plateau herbicide, wildflower mixes, and more.

MISSOURI WILDFLOWERS NURSERY
   9814 Pleasant Hill Road
   Jefferson City, MO 65109
   (573)496-3492; fax, (573)496-3003
   mowldflrs@sockets.net
   Offers more than 175 species of native perennial seeds and plants. Seed sold by packet, ounce, or pound.

ROCK POST WILDFLOWERS NURSERY
   5798 Windy Meadows Lane
   Fulton, MO 65251
   (573)642-6927
   mike-ann@sockets.net
   Offers bare-root and potted forbs, grasses, and trees but no seeds.

SHARP BROTHERS SEED CO.
   396 SW Davis–LaDue
   Clinton, MO 64735
   (800)451-3779, (660)885-7551; fax, (660)885-8647
   Native grass and wildflower seeds.

Wisconsin

AGRECOL
   www.agrecol.com
   1984 Berlin Road
   Sun Prairie, WI 53590
   (608)897-8547
   Offers seeds, plants, and contract growing for prairies, wetlands, and savannas.

APPLIED ECOLOGICAL SERVICES, INC., AND TAYLOR CREEK NURSERY
   Route 3, Smith Road
   P.O. Box 256
   Bordhead, WI 53520
   (608)897-8641
   Offers prairie, woodland, and wetland plants; consultation; installation; and burning.

AQUATIC RESOURCES AND GLACIAL POND
FARMS
P.O. Box 2221
Wausau, WI 54402
(715)845-2099
Offers prairie and wetland species.

BLUESTEM FARM
S5920 Lehman Road
Baraboo, WI 53913
(608)356-0179
Offers plants, consultation.

CRM ECOSYSTEMS
9738 Overland Road
Mount Horeb, WI 53572
(608)437-5245
Consulting, restoration, and management.

COUNTRY WETLANDS NURSERY
Box 126
Muskego, WI 53150
(414)679-1268
*Offers wetland, prairie, and woodland
plants and seeds; consultation; design; and
management.*

DRAGONFLY GARDENS
P.O. Box 192
Amery, WI 54001
(715)268-6155
Offers prairie plants and nonnative plants.

A GROWING CONCERN
4990 West Donna Drive
Brown Deer, WI 53223
(414)354-1638
Offers prairie and woodland species.

HILD & ASSOCIATES
www.hildnatives.com
326 Glover Road South
River Falls, WI 54022
(715)426-5131; fax, (715)426-9887
ghild@hildnatives.com
*Offers wholesale prairie and wetland plants
for restoration.*

J & J TRANZPLANT AQUATIC NURSERY
P.O. Box 227
Wild Rose, WI 54984-0227
(715)256-0059; fax, (715)256-0039
*Offers Wisconsin-ecotype woodland, wetland,
and prairie plants and seeds.*

KETTLE MORAINE NATURAL LANDSCAPING
W996 Birchwood Drive
Campbellsport, WI 53010
(414)533-8939
*Offers east-central Wisconsin-ecotype prairie
seeds.*

LITTLE VALLEY FARM
Route 3, Box 544
Snead Creek Road
Spring Green, WI 53588
(608)935-3324
Offers prairie and woodland seeds and plants.

MIDWEST PRAIRIES
Fort Atkinson, WI
(920)563-3165
Offers Wisconsin-ecotype plants and seeds.

MURN ENVIRONMENTAL, INC.
10282 Riverview Drive
Edgerton, WI 53534
(414)473-2737, (608)884-6563
*Offers seeds of native prairie, wetland, and
woodland plants.*

NATURE'S NURSERY
6125 Mathewson Road
Mazomanie, WI 53560
(608)795-4920
*Offers southern Wisconsin ecotypes of prairie,
woodland, and wetland seeds and plants.*

OAK PRAIRIE FARMS
Pardeeville, WI
(800)894-3884
Offers Wisconsin-ecotype plants and seeds.

L. L. OLDS SEED CO.
Madison, WI
(800)356-7333
Offers Wisconsin-ecotype seeds.

PLANTSCAPES
Madison, WI
(608)223-3564, (800)807-7526
Offers Wisconsin-ecotype plants.

PRAIRIE FUTURE SEED CO.
P.O. Box 644
Menomonee Falls, WI 53052
(414)246-4019
Offers Wisconsin-ecotype plants and seeds.

PRAIRIE FRONTIER
www.prairiefrontier.com
W 281 S 3606 Pheasant Run
Waukesha, WI 53189
(414)544-6708
Offers plants and seeds.

PRAIRIE NURSERY, INC.
prairienursery.com
P.O. Box 306
Westfield, WI 53964
(800)476-9453
Fax, (608)296-2741
*Offers plants and seeds, landscaping, and
consulting services.*

PRAIRIE RIDGE NURSERY
RR 2
9738 Overland Road
Mount Horeb, WI 53572
(608)437-5245
Fax, (608)437-2832
*Offers prairie, wetland, and woodland
seeds and plants, as well as installation and
management.*

PRAIRIE SEED SOURCE
P.O. Box 83
North Lake, WI 53064
(414)673-7166
*Offers southeast Wisconsin ecotypes of prairie
and savanna species.*

RETZER NATURE CENTER
W284 S1530 Road DT
Waukesha, WI 53188
(414)521-5407
*Offers local-ecotype seed and plants for
projects within 50 miles of Waukesha County
line.*

ROHDE'S NURSERY
N8098 Duck Creek Avenue
Neshkoro, WI 54960
(414)293-4373
*Offers prairie, wetland, and woodland
plants, as well as design, installation, and
consultation.*

WEHR NATURE CENTER
9107 West College Avenue
Franklin, WI 53132
(414)425-8550
*Offers prairie seeds and instruction for small
projects in southeastern Wisconsin.*

WILDLIFE NURSERIES, INC.
P.O. Box 2724
Oshkosh, WI 54903
Offers native wetland plant materials.

Books of Interest

AMERICAN WILDLIFE AND PLANTS, A GUIDE TO WILDLIFE FOOD HABITS

Alexander Martin, Herbert Zim, and Arnold Nelson

In this book organized by both plant and animal, the reader can, for example, look under "rose breasted grosbeak" to find its major food sources or look up a list of plants, both native and introduced, that attract hummingbirds. Likewise, under entries for such plants as Jack-in the-pulpit or oak can be found a list of animals that use it for a food source. Although this book does not include butterflies or other insects, it does include birds, mammals, fish, amphibians, and reptiles.

A FIELD GUIDE TO WILDFLOWERS OF NORTH-EASTERN AND NORTH-CENTRAL AMERICA (PETERSON FIELD GUIDE SERIES)

Roger Tory Peterson and Margaret McKermy

This book is a no-nonsense field guide to wildflower identification. Organized by flower color, the text contains no extraneous information, just what is needed for certain identification of a species. Clear line drawings of leaf and flower point out unique features to look for when trying to identify a plant. It includes both native and introduced species.

FERNS FOR AMERICAN GARDENS

John T. Mickel

This book includes cultural information and clear color photographs of just about any fern that might be used in the home landscape. It can be used for field identification of ferns as well.

INVASIVE PLANTS, WEEDS OF THE GLOBAL GARDEN

John M. Randall and Janet Marinelli, editors

This clear, user-friendly guide—from the Brooklyn Botanic Garden—for identifying and controlling invasive plants that threaten wild areas across the United States contains large, full-color photographs and extensive information on each plant listed.

LANDSCAPING WITH NATIVE TREES: THE NORTHEAST, MIDWEST, MIDSOUTH AND SOUTHEAST EDITION

Guy Sternberg and Jim Wilson

Written by two experienced plantsmen, Jim Wilson of Georgia and Guy Sternberg of Illinois, this book is full of great color photographs and interesting information on trees native to the eastern United States.

MAN AND NATURE: OR, PHYSICAL GEOGRAPHY AS MODIFIED BY HUMAN ACTION

George P. Marsh

First published in 1864 and written by a Vermonter concerned with how agricultural practices inappropriate to the state's hilly terrain were seriously degrading the natural environment, the book outlines an early conservationist ethic and is said to have inspired Aldo Leopold.

MANUAL OF WOODY LANDSCAPE PLANTS

Michael A. Dirr

Covering hundreds of trees and shrubs used in the eastern United States, this book is the granddaddy of all woody plant landscape manuals and can be found in the library of most landscape architects and horticulturists. Containing illustrative line drawings, it is written so that needed information can be found easily.

PLANTING NOAH'S GARDEN: FURTHER ADVENTURES IN BACKYARD ECOLOGY

Sara B. Stein

This book enumerates the trials and tribulations of a homeowner's adventure into native landscaping, offering insights on the process and possibilities of using native plants around the home. Written as a series of short essays, it is enjoyable reading.

PLANTS OF THE CHICAGO REGION
Floyd Swink and Gerould Wilhelm
This book is one of the most important for those interested in identifying midwestern native plants, their natural associations with other plants, and the habitats where they are commonly found. This tome also describes introduced species. It is written in an encyclopedic manner with no photographs or illustrations; packed with nearly 5 pounds of information, it is a great reference book but not the most portable field guide.

A SAND COUNTY ALMANAC
Aldo Leopold
Written by a forester turned ecologist, this book was first published in 1949 and continues to inspire those interested in preserving our country's natural beauty. The book is a collection of short essays on the observations of the natural world and of how human actions can thoughtlessly destroy entire ecosystems solely for economic gain. *A Sand County Almanac* brought to popular attention the need for a "land ethic."

TALLGRASS PRAIRIE WILDFLOWERS
Doug Ladd
Offers large color photographs of almost 300 commonly encountered prairie wildflowers and grasses. Although not an extensive field guide, it makes an excellent introduction to the beauty and variety of prairie plants.

Useful Web Sites

WILD ONES—NATURAL LANDSCAPERS, LTD.
www.for-wild.org
Wild Ones is a national, nonprofit organization that promotes landscaping with native plants, with local chapters around the country. *The Wild Ones Handbook* on the use of native plants in the home landscape is posted on their Web site.

GRAND PRAIRIE FRIENDS OF ILLINOIS
www.grandprairiefriends.org
A nonprofit group in east-central Illinois, GPF is concerned with preserving and restoring tall-grass prairie. The site contains a wide range of information on the tallgrass prairie, an extensive list of commercial native plant sources, contact information for plant experts and native plant societies, as well as a calendar of events and numerous links to other useful sites concerning prairies and native plant landscaping.

THE TALLGRASS PRAIRIE OF ILLINOIS
www.inhs.illinois.edu/~kenr/tallgrass.html
This Web site is hosted by the Illinois Natural History Survey and created by Ken Robertson, a prairie enthusiast and botanist for the survey. The site contains a history and description of the diversity of the tallgrass prairie, images, and botanical information on most prairie plants, as well as many links to other interesting sites.

INDIANA NATIVE PLANT AND WILDFLOWER SOCIETY
www.inpaws.org
The INPAWS site contains a descriptive list with images of plants that threaten wild areas in and around Indiana. It also has a section on landscaping with native plants and a list of native plant sources.

GARDENWEB
www.gardenweb.com
GardenWeb hosts a seed exchange and a long list of gardening/plant forums, including one on wildflowers and native plants. It also lists nonprofit plant societies, clubs, botanical gardens, and other organizations.

WOODY PLANTS DATABASE
woodyplants.nres.uiuc.edu
Hosted by the University of Illinois Department of Natural Resources and Environmental Sciences, this site allows the user to search its database for cultural and descriptive information on trees and shrubs used in landscaping. The information includes images and descriptions of the plant's growth habit, bark, flower, fruit, leaves, buds, stems, and fall color.

THE PRAIRIE ENTHUSIASTS
www.theprairieenthusiasts.org
This grassroots organization is concerned with the maintenance and recovery of the tallgrass prairie and oak savanna ecosystems of Wisconsin and northern Illinois. The site includes a forum where native plant and restoration questions can be discussed, lists of tallgrass prairie plants and associated wildlife native to Wisconsin, and a calendar of events.

SILVICS OF NORTH AMERICA
www.na.fs.fed.us/spfo/pubs/silvics_manual/table_of_contents.htm
An updated guide to conifers and hardwood trees originally published in 1986 by the USDA Forest Service. Covering over 200 native and introduced species, the guide describes a tree's growth rate, habit, and cultural requirements, as well as its historic range, value to wildlife, and potential disease or insect problems.

Bibliography

Armstrong, Patricia. "Planting a Prairie in an Urban Yard: Design, Installation, and Management." (Presentation, Natural Landscaping Seminar, 2001. Crystal Lake, Illinois, February 24, 2001.) *(Chapter 6)*

Art, Henry W. *The Wildflower Gardener's Guide.* (Pownal, Vermont: Garden Way Publishing, 1994.) *(Chapters 1, 4, 6)*

Art, Henry W. "To Spray or Not to Spray," in *Invasive Plants. Weeds of the Global Garden,* handbook no. 149, ed. John M. Randall and Janet Marinelli. (Brooklyn: Brooklyn Botanic Garden Inc., 1996.) *(Chapter 6)*

Betz, Robert F. "What Is a Prairie," in *The Prairie, Swell and Swale.* (Dundee, Illinois: Torkel Korling Publishing, 1972.) *(Chapter 1)*

Blaser, Werner. *Architecture and Nature, the Work of Alfred Caldwell.* (Boston: Birkhauser Verlag Publishing, 1984.)

Brooks, John. *Natural Landscapes.* (London: DK Publishing, 1998.)

Brooks, Thomas. "Natural Landscaping, A Guide to Creating Natural Looking Landscapes in the Prairie State." (Master's thesis, University of Illinois, Department of Landscape Architecture, 1992.)

Bryson, Reid A., David A. Baerreis, and Wayne M. Wendland. "The Character of Late-Glacial and Post-Glacial Climatic Changes," in *Pleistocene and Recent Environments of the Central Great Plains,* ed. Wakefield Dort, Jr., and J. Knox Jones, Jr., 54–74. (Lawrence: The University Press of Kansas, 1970.) *(Chapter 1)*

Cathey, H. Marc. *Selecting, Planting, and Caring for Trees.* (Alexandria, Virginia: American Horticultural Society, 2000.) *(Chapter 6)*

Chicago Park District. *Chicago Park District Annual Report for 1937.* (Chicago, 1937.)

Chicago Public Library. *Chicago Timeline, 1837 Incorporated as a City.* (http://cpl.lib.uic.edu/004chicago/timeline/inc.html, accessed February 16, 2001.) *(Chapter 1)*

Chicago Region Biodiversity Council. *Biodiversity Recovery Plan.* (Chicago: Chicago Region Biodiversity Council, 1999.) *(Chapter 2)*

Coder, Kim D. "Tree Quality BMP's for Developing Wooded Areas and Protecting Residual Trees," in *Trees and Planting Sites,* ed. Gary W. Watson. (Savoy, Illinois: International Society of Arboriculture, 1995.) *(Chapters 3, 4)*

Craul, Phillip J. *Urban Soil in Landscape Design.* (New York: John Wiley & Sons, Inc., 1992.) *(Chapters 3, 6)*

DeFreitas, Stan. *The Water-Thrifty Garden.* (Dallas: Taylor Publishing Company, 1993.) *(Chapter 2)*

DeHorn, Jim. Member of Treekeepers. Chicago: personal communication, May 17, 2000. *(Chapter 6)*

Diblik, Roy. Presentation on using native plants in the designed landscape. (Illinois Landscape Contractor's Association Seminar. Hoffman Estates, Illinois, January 14, 2000.) *(Chapter 6)*

Diboll, Neil. "Removing Vegetation," in *Wild Ones Handbook.* (Milwaukee: Wild Ones—Natural Landscapers, Ltd., 1997.) *(Chapter 6)*

Dirr, Michael A. *Manual of Woody Landscape Plants: Their Identification, Ornamental Characteristics, Culture, Propagation and Uses.* (Champaign, Illinois: Stipes Publishing Company, 1990.) *(Chapter 4)*

Domer, Dennis. *Alfred Caldwell, The Life and Work of a Prairie School Landscape Architect.* (Baltimore: Johns Hopkins University Press, 1997.)

Dort, Wakefield, Jr., and J. Knox Jones, Jr. *Pleistocene and Recent Environments of the Central Great Plains.* (Lawrence: The University Press of Kansas, 1970.)

Dreeszen, Vincent H. "The Stratigraphic Framework of Pleistocene Glacial and Periglacial Deposits in the Central Great Plains" in *Pleistocene and Recent Environments of the*

Central Great Plains, ed. Wakefield Dort, Jr., and J. Knox Jones, Jr., 9–22. (Lawrence: The University Press of Kansas, 1970.)

Eaton, Leonard. *Landscape Artist in America.* (Chicago: University of Chicago Press, 1964.)

Elias, Thomas S. *The Complete Trees of North America: A Field Guide and Natural History.* (New York: Gramercy Publishing Company, 1987.) *(Chapter 4)*

Ellis, Barbara W., ed. *Rodale's Illustrated Encyclopedia of Gardening and Landscape Techniques.* (Emmaus, Pennsylvania: Rodale Press, 1990.) *(Chapters 3, 6)*

Environmental Protection Agency, United States. EPA-420-F-96-018 fact sheet. (EPA Task Group on Environmentally and Economically Beneficial Landscaping, 1996.) *(Chapter 2)*

Environmental Protection Agency, United States. *Landscaping with Native Plants.* (March 1999.) *(Chapter 2)*

Francis, Mark, and Andreas Reiman. *The California Landscape Garden.* (Berkeley: University of California Press, 1999.) *(Chapter 2)*

Gleason, Henry Allan. "The Flora of the Prairies." (Bachelor's thesis, University of Illinois, 1901.) *(Chapter 1)*

Gleason, Henry A., and Arthur Cronquist. *Manual of Vascular Plants of Northeastern United States and Adjacent Canada.* (Bronx: The New York Botanical Garden, 1995.) *(Chapter 4)*

Green, Thomas L., and Peggy Young. "Parkway Tree Protection Program," in *Trees and Planting Sites,* ed. Gary W. Watson. (Savoy, Illinois: International Society of Arboriculture, 1995.) *(Chapter 6)*

Hall, James. *Notes on the Western States.* (Philadelphia: Harrison Hall, 1838.) *(Chapter 1)*

Harkness, Terrence. "Garden from Region," in *The Meaning of Gardens. Idea, Place and Action,* ed. Mark Francis and Randolph T. Hester, Jr., 118–122. (Cambridge: The MIT Press, 1991.)

Harstad, Carolyn. *Go Native! Gardening with Native Plants and Wildflowers in the Lower Midwest.* (Indianapolis: Indiana University Press, 1999.) *(Chapter 4)*

Hassett, John J., and Wayne L. Banwart. *Soils and Their Environment.* (Englewood Cliffs, New Jersey: Prentice Hall, 1992.) *(Chapter 3)*

Hightshoe, Gary L. *Native Trees, Shrubs, and Vines for Urban and Rural America.* (New York: Van Nostrand Reinhold Company, 1988.) *(Chapter 4)*

Illinois Natural History Survey. *Fieldbook of Illinois Wild Flowers.* (Urbana: Natural History Survey Division, 1936.) *(Chapter 4)*

International Society of Arboriculture. *New Tree Planting.* (Champaign, Illinois: 1995.) *(Chapter 6)*

Johnson, Lorraine. *100 Easy-to-Grow Native Plants for American Gardens in Temperate Zones.* (Buffalo, New York: Firefly Books Inc., 1999.) *(Chapter 4)*

Jones, Samual B., and Leonard E. Foote. *Gardening with Native Wild Flowers.* (Portland, Oregon: Timber Press, 1990.)

Joyce, David, with John Elsley as U.S. consultant. *The Perfect Plant for Every Site, Habitat, and Garden Style.* (New York: Stewart, Tabori & Chang, 1998.) *(Chapter 4)*

King, James E. "The Prairies of Illinois," *The Living Museum,* vol. 43, no. 4 (1981). *(Chapter 1)*

Ladd, Doug. *Tallgrass Prairie Wildflowers, A Field Guide.* (Helena, Montana: Falcon Publishing Inc., 1995.) *(Chapter 4)*

Leopold, Aldo. *A Sand County Almanac.* (New York: Ballantine Books, Inc., 1970.) *(Chapters 2, 3)*

Mclure, Susan. *Midwest Landscape Design.* (Dallas: Taylor Publishing Company, 1999.)

Martin, Alexander C., Herbert S. Zim, and Arnold L. Nelson. *American Wildlife and Plants: A Guide to Wildlife Food Habits.* (New York: Dover Publications Inc., 1961.) *(Chapter 4)*

Mason, Sandra. "Mulching Trees," in *Homeowner's Column.* (University of Illinois Extension—Champaign County: June 20, 1998.) *(Chapter 6)*

Mason, Sandra. "Practicing Correct Tree Planting" in *Homeowner's Column.* (University of Illinois Extension—Champaign County: March 25, 2000.) *(Chapter 6)*

McClain, William E. *Prairie Establishment and Landscaping,* technical publication no. 2. (Springfield: Division of Natural Heritage, Illinois Department of Natural Resources, 1997.) *(Chapters 1, 6)*

McFall, Don, and Jean Karnes, ed. *A Directory of Illinois Nature Preserves,* vol. 1. (Springfield: Illinois Department of Natural Resources, 1995.) *(Chapter 1)*

Mickel, John T. *Ferns for American Gardens.* (New York: Macmillan Publishing Company, 1994.) *(Chapter 4)*

Midewin National Tallgrass Prairie, Openlands. *Midewin Timeline.* (http://www.openlands.org/midewin/timeline.html, accessed February 4, 2001.) *(Chapter 1)*

Miller, Wilhelm. *The "Illinois Way" of Beautifying the Farm,* University of Illinois circular 170. (Urbana: University of Illinois Press, 1914.)

Miller, Wilhelm. *The Prairie Spirit in Landscape Gardening,* University of Illinois circular 184. (Urbana: University of Illinois Press, 1915.)

Mish, Frederick C., ed. *Webster's Ninth New Collegiate Dictionary.* (Springfield, Massachusetts: Merriam Webster Inc., 1986.) *(Chapter 4)*

Mohlenbrock, Robert H. *Forest Trees of Illinois.* (Springfield: Illinois Department of Conservation, 1973.) *(Chapter 4)*

Mohlenbrock, Robert H. *The Illustrated Flora of Illinois. Ferns.* (Carbondale: Southern Illinois University Press, 1967.) *(Chapter 4)*

Mohlenbrock, Robert H. "Sedges: Carex," in *The Illustrated Flora of Illinois.* (Carbondale: Southern Illinois University Press, 1999.) *(Chapter 4)*

Mohlenbrock, Robert H., and Douglas M. Ladd. *Distribution of Illinois Vascular Plants.* (Carbondale: Southern Illinois University Press, 1978.)

Natura, Heidi. *Root Systems of Prairie Plants.* (Elmhurst, Illinois: Conservation Design Forum, Inc., 1995.) *(Chapter 2)*

Neil, Bill. *Gardener's Latin.* (Chapel Hill, North Carolina: Algonquin Books, 1992.) *(Chapter 4)*

Niering, William A. *The Audubon Society Field Guide to North American Wildflowers: Eastern Region.* (New York: Alfred A. Knopf, 1979.) *(Chapter 4)*

Northeastern Illinois Planning Commission. *Source Book on Natural Landscaping for Local Officials,* publication 1998-648-189. (U.S. Government Printing Office, August 1998.) *(Chapter 2)*

Ottesen, Carole. *The Native Plant Primer.* (New York: Harmony Books, 1995.) *(Chapter 4)*

Packard, Stephen. "Living with Nature: Wilderness in your Yard." (Presentation, Natural Landscaping Seminar. Crystal Lake, Illinois, February 24, 2001.) *(Chapters 1, 6)*

Peattie, Donald Culross. *A Natural History of Trees of Eastern and Central North America.* (Boston: Houghton Mifflin Company, 1950. *(Chapter 4)*

Phillips, Harry R. *Growing and Propagating Wild Flowers.* (Chapel Hill: The University of North Carolina Press, 1985.) *(Chapter 4)*

Pielou, E. C. *After the Ice Age, The Return of Life to Glaciated North America.* (Chicago: The University of Chicago Press, 1992.) *(Chapter 1)*

Robertson, Kenneth R. "The Tallgrass Prairie." *Plant Talk,* January 2000. *(Chapter 1)*

Ruhe, Robert V. "Soils, Paleosols, and the Environment," in *Pleistocene and Recent Environments of the Central Great Plains,* ed. Wakefield Dort, Jr., and J. Knox Jones, Jr., 37–54. (Lawrence: The University Press of Kansas, 1970.)

Runkel, Sylvan T., and Alvin F. Bull. *Wildflowers of Illinois Woodlands.* (Ames: Iowa State University Press, 1994.) *(Chapter 4)*

Schuberth, Christopher J. A *View of the Past, An Introduction to Illinois Geology.* (Springfield: Illinois State Museum, 1986.) *(Chapter 1)*

Shaw, Connor. "The Myth and Reality of Native Oaks," *The Weedpatch Gazette.* (Richmond, Illinois: Winter 2000.) *(Chapters 4, 6)*

Shaw, Connor. "Native Woody Trees and Shrubs to be Used in the Landscape." (Presentation, Natural Landscaping Seminar, 2001, Crystal Lake, Illinois, February 24, 2001.)

Smith, J. Robert, and Beatrice S. Smith. *The Prairie Garden, 70 Native Plants You Can Grow in Town or Country.* (Madison: The University of Wisconsin Press, 1980.) *(Chapter 4)*

Spencer, Edwin Rollin. *All About Weeds.* (New York: Dover Publications, Inc., 1974.

Stannard, Lewis J. "On the Origin and Maintenance of the Tallgrass Prairie." *Erigenia*, no. 4 (August 1984). (Carbondale, Illinois: Southern Illinois Native Plant Society.) *(Chapter 1)*

Starbuck, Chris. "Mulch—The Good, the Bad, and the Ugly," *City Trees*, vol. 35, no. 6. (St. Louis: The Society of Municipal Arborists, November/December 1999.) *(Chapter 6)*

Stein, Sara. *Noah's Garden.* (New York: Houghton Mifflin, 1993.) *(Chapter 3)*

Sternberg, Guy, and Jim Wilson. *Landscaping with Native Trees, The Northeast, Midwest, Midsouth and Southeast Edition.* (Shelburne, Vermont: Chapters Publishing Ltd., 1995.) *(Chapter 4)*

Stokes, Donald, and Lillian Stokes. *Stokes Wildflower Book: The Complete Guide to Growing and Identifying Wildflowers East of the Rockies.* (Boston: Little, Brown and Company, 1992.) *(Chapter 4)*

Swink, Floyd, and Gerould Wilhelm. *Plants of the Chicago Region*, 4th edition. (Indianapolis: Indiana Academy of Science, 1994.) *(Chapter 3)*

Taylor, Patricia A. *Easy Care Native Plants.* (New York: Henry Holt and Company, 1996.)

Tehon, Leo R. *Fieldbook of Native Illinois Shrubs.* (Urbana: Natural History Survey Division, 1942.)

Tishler, William H., ed. *American Landscape Architecture, Designers and Places.* (Washington, D.C.: The Preservation Press, 1989.)

Walsh, Michelle Byrne. "Five Steps to Prairie Establishment," *The Landscape Contractor.* (May 2000.) *(Chapter 2)*

Watson, Gary W., ed. *Selecting and Planting Trees.* (Lisle, Illinois: The Morton Arboretum, 1992.) *(Chapters 3, 6)*

Watts, May T. *Reading the Landscape, An Adventure in Ecology.* (New York: The Macmillan Company, 1967.) *(Chapters 1, 3)*

Weaver, J.E. *North American Prairie.* (Lincoln, Nebraska: Johnsen Publishing Company, 1954.) *(Chapter 1)*

Weaver, J. E. *Prairie Plants and Their Environment, A Fifty-Year Study in the Midwest.* (Lincoln: University of Nebraska Press, 1968.) *(Chapter 2)*

Wiggers, Raymond. *Geology Underfoot in Illinois.* (Missoula, Montana: Mountain Press Publishing Company, 1997.) *(Chapter 1)*

Wilson, Jim. *Landscaping with Wildflowers. An Environmental Approach to Gardening.* (Boston: Houghton Mifflin Company, 1992.) *(Chapters 2, 6)*

Index

Credits

Photographs

Michael R. Jeffords: pages 11, left; 12; 26, bottom; 29, bottom; 32, top; 33, middle; 34, bottom; 35; 40, bottom; 43, top; 45, bottom; 47, top; 49; 54, bottom; 55, bottom.

Gary J. Kling: pages iv, bottom; 10; 11, right; 22, top; 46; 51, top; 52; 53, top and middle; 54, top; 55, top and middle; 60, middle; 62, top; 63, bottom; 64, top three and bottom; 72; 73, bottom.

Keith Nowakowski: pages 22, middle and bottom; 24, left; 25, top; 26, top, inset; 29, top; 30, bottom; 31, top; 32, bottom; 33, top and bottom; 36; 37, top; 38, bottom; 48; 56; 57, bottom; 61, bottom; 62, middle.

Robert J. Reber: pages 41, top; 42; 43, bottom; 74.

David Riecks: pages iv, top; 24, inset; 25, bottom; 27, top; 31, bottom; 34, top; 37, bottom; 38, top; 39; 40, top; 44; 45, top; 47, bottom; 50; 51, bottom; 53, bottom; 57, top; 58; 59; 60, top and bottom; 61; 62, bottom; 63, top; 64, second from bottom; 65 to 71; 73, top.

Kenneth R. Robertson: pages 7; 27, bottom; 28; 30, top; 41, bottom.

Front cover: top, prairie dropseed, Riecks; background, prairie dropseed, Robertson; grid inset: bloodroot, Reber; prairie dropseed, Robertson; river birch, Riecks; sugar maple, Kling; white pine, Riecks; eastern redbud, Kling; prairie smoke, Jeffords; aromatic aster, Robertson; gray dogwood, Kling. *Title page (i):* woodland perennial grouping of woodland ginger, Christmas fern, and Jacob's ladder; Riecks. *Title page reverse (ii):* columbine, Riecks. *Back cover:* top, prairie dropseed, Riecks; inset: woodland perennial grouping of woodland ginger, Christmas fern, and Jacob's ladder, Riecks; butterfly milkweed, Riecks; prairie trillium, Jeffords.

Illustrations

Keith Nowakowski

Production

This publication was produced by staff members in Information Technology and Communications Services of the College of Agricultural, Consumer and Environmental Sciences.

Editor: Mary Overmier
Designer: Kathleen Chmelewski
Staff Photographer: David Riecks
Proofreader: Erin Cler